Colin McEvedy The Penguin
Atlas of
Ancient History

Maps devised by the author
and drawn by John Woodcock

Penguin Books

Penguin Books Ltd, Harmondsworth,
Middlesex, England
Penguin Books, 625 Madison Avenue,
New York, New York 10022, U.S.A.
Penguin Books Australia Ltd, Ringwood,
Victoria, Australia
Penguin Books Canada Ltd,
41 Steelcase Road West,
Markham, Ontario, Canada
Penguin Books (N.Z.) Ltd,
182–190 Wairau Road,
Auckland 10, New Zealand

First published 1967
Reprinted 1968, 1970, 1972, 1975 (twice), 1976
Copyright © Colin McEvedy, 1967

Printed in Great Britain by
Fletcher & Son Ltd, Norwich
Set in Monotype Times

# Contents

# Introduction

This atlas has the same general aims as the companion volume on Medieval History already published as a Penguin: the thesis behind it is that there is a valid unit of study in the area comprised by Europe, the southern coast of the Mediterranean and the Near East. Accordingly, the geographical framework is held constant and the changes of people and state are projected on this background in a series of diagrams of constant scale. The book is, I hope, sufficiently well ordered to be useful as a work of reference, but its primary purpose is to present as a coherent story the origin and evolution of the historic cultures of Europe and the Near East up to the fourth century A.D.

Every account of mankind's first literate societies begins with a description of the fertile crescent – the arc of arable land passing from Palestine through Syria to Mesopotamia; the equivalent in histories of classical antiquity is the term Mediterranean World which includes the Palestinian/Syrian segment of the fertile crescent. Mesopotamia was by then under the political domination of the Iranians and throughout the classical period the Iranian plateau was the site of a power comparable to those of the Mediterranean in scale and social organization. Our Graeco-Roman cultural bias may neglect the Achaemenid, Parthian and Sassanid states but the Mediterranean and Iranian polities really form a single if bilobed unit; attempts to treat them separately must always be artificial for their interaction was constant.

As the barbarian neighbours of an empire are among its primary concerns, so its interests stretch to the limits of significant settlement. For the Roman Empire these limits are the Arctic Circle, the Atlantic and the Sahara. The Persian sphere includes Transoxiana and the Indus valley; its borders are the Arabian Sea in the south and

3

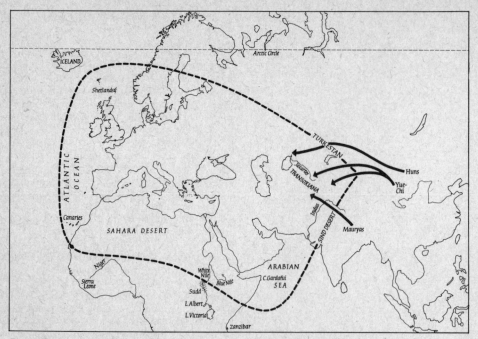

*Fig. 1.* The Europe–Near East area in ancient times and the movement into it of the Mauryas (third century B.C.), Yue-Chi (second century B.C.) and Huns (first century A.D.).

the wastes of Turkestan and the desert of Sind in the west (see Fig. 1). Taking the two areas together, the validity of the northern, western and southern borders (Arctic Circle–Atlantic Ocean–Sahara Desert–Arabian Sea) can hardly be disputed; of the myriad movements of historical importance in the period under consideration not one transgressed these limits.

The eastern border cannot be given the same definitive character, for there were undeniably important relationships between the inhabitants of the Near East on the one hand and of further Asia and India on the other. But, politically speaking, these relations were exceptional and

infrequent. After the expansion of the Iranians into India and Asia in the second millennium B.C. no western-based power ever extended significantly beyond the Jaxartes or Indus; conversely, only two peoples, the Yue-Chi in the second century B.C. and the Huns in the first century A.D., entered Western Asia from the East. In India the desert of Sind was only crossed once, in the fourth century B.C. by the Mauryas who temporarily incorporated the Indus valley in their empire. Provided these exceptions are noted the Europe–Near East area can be regarded as effectively isolated politically from both Central Asia and India east of the Sind Desert.

The area covered by the base-map used in the atlas (Fig. 2) has limits that correspond with this theoretical outline and, except in the east, with the geographical knowledge of the ancients. In the north it over-states Mediterranean information on the Scandinavian peninsula which was regarded as an island; half of Iceland gets in, an ambivalence that reflects a genuine uncertainty, for scholars debate whether the island of Thule that lay six days' sail to the north of Scotland was Iceland or Norway (it was probably only the Shetlands, for distances beyond the periphery of usual travel tended to be wildly overestimated). On the western side as much of the Atlantic coastline of Africa is shown as came under the influence of the Mediterranean world. The occasional ship went further; the Canaries were certainly visited and there is a record of an exploratory voyage reaching Sierra Leone; but the Canaries were not occupied and the brief contact with Black Africa did not lead to any regular traffic. Neither does there appear to have been any significant trade across the Sahara though the Romans gained a hearsay knowledge of the Niger in its middle, eastward flowing, section. It was speculated that this might be the upper Nile, the course of which was known only as far as the confluence of its White and Blue branches; perhaps it traversed the Sahara from west to east before turning north in Upper Nubia? Nero sent two centurions to Egypt with orders to try and solve the problem; they travelled up the White Nile to the point where it emerges from the impenetrable swamps now called the Sudd. This left matters much where they were and, in fact, no one got any further until 1842.

The lower edge of the base-map crosses the northern margin of the Sudd; further east it cuts the coast of Africa some 600 miles south of Cape Gardafui, which corresponds to the limit of normal trade contacts in Roman times. Zanzibar was known to a few hardy seamen but this was the limit (no notice should be taken of a tall tale

4

about the circumnavigation of Africa in the time of the Pharaoh Necho). The contact with Zanzibar in the end brought information about the interior which suggested the true solution of the Nile problem; Ptolemy's map of A.D. 150 shows the river rising in the Mountains of the Moon (the Ruwenzori range?) and flowing north via two large lakes that will do for Victoria and Albert.

The right-hand border of the map corresponds with the political limits of the Europe–Near East area, but as trade with India and China was steady throughout the classical period, the geographical information available to the ancients goes far beyond this line. The direction and extent of the Asian land mass was perceived and the larger details – the island of Ceylon, the Malay peninsula – could be roughed in. The size of the continent was overestimated by about forty per cent, an exaggeration that was still current in the fifteenth century and, together with an underestimate of the size of the globe, encouraged Columbus in his attempt to reach China via the Atlantic.

The geographical area defined is a valid unit of study in that it contains all the interacting elements of a closed system. The next stage is analytical and concerns the elements that take part in the reactions – the peoples of the Europe–Near East area.

A race is a population that has been isolated sufficiently long to have developed characteristics that distinguish its members from those of the same species but different provenance. The area within which the race evolved is its ecosphere. The borders of an ecosphere are either barriers of a physical type – such as seas or mountains – or zones where there is a change in environment – such as a transition from arable land to desert. The Europe–Near East area as defined is the ecosphere of the white race, as Africa south of the Sahara is that of the black, China of the

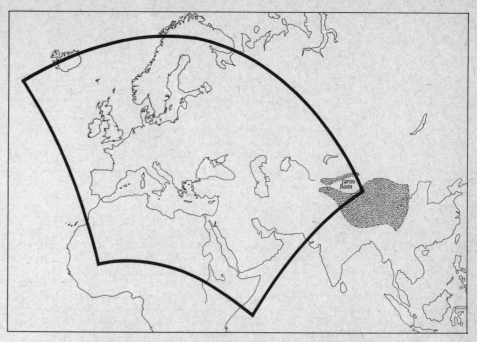

Fig. 2. The area shown on the base-map, superimposed on the Mercator projection used in Fig. 1. The base-map uses a conical projection with the result that its right-hand border in its upper part is pointing markedly more east than north. As can be seen by comparing this map with Fig. 3 the rotation is maximal in the upper right-hand corner, the area of the Tarim Basin and Central Asian massif.

yellow and India of the Dravidian. Each of these major races and ecospheres can be divided into sub-races with correspondingly smaller ecospheres. The important subdivisions of the white race are the Semites occupying the Arabian peninsula, the Hamites occupying Africa north and east of the Sahara, the Indo-Europeans occupying arable continental Europe and the Finns occupying the northern forest zone. As far as we know, the Semitic, Hamitic and Finnish peoples evolved *in situ* from the earliest postglacial inhabitants of the Arabian, North African and North Eurasian ecospheres; but the Indo-

Europeans, expanding from an Eastern European homeland, overran and absorbed at least two other peoples: one at the western end of the Mediterranean and one in Asia Minor. These two groups, the West Mediterranean and the Caucasian, are currently represented by the Basques of the Pyrenees and the Georgians of the Caucasus. We have thus six groups that we can consider as autochthonous for our area.

Before considering these peoples in detail we must note that the mode of definition has changed as we pass from race to sub-race. There is some basis in physical features for sub-racial distinctions,

5

but the overlap is too great to allow the individual to be placed with certainty. We can distinguish a hundred Scandinavians from a hundred Spaniards by observing the percentage of blonds but not, with any degree of certainty, one Scandinavian from one Spaniard. Even when we have refined our genetic techniques we will probably never be able to place geographically groups smaller than ten. Sub-racial characteristics are accordingly characteristics of the community not of the individual. Once we realize that we are considering the classification of human communities we have no reason to be limited to purely physical measurements but can take social behaviour as our index, and though for most aspects of social behaviour we lack an adequate system of notation, for language we possess not only this but also an immense amount of analysable information. The study of language enables us to draw up a genetic tree for our sub-racial communities: as Dr Johnson said 'Languages are the pedigrees of nations'.[1]

Now let us consider the sub-races in turn with appropriate linguistic comment. Semitic and Hamitic are related; but whereas the Semitic languages form a true group, Hamitic is a partly geographical concept in that the major members are as closely related to Semitic as they are to each other. This is reasonable, for the Hamitic ecosphere divides naturally into three zones – the Moghreb (Morocco–Algeria–Tunisia), Egypt and Abyssinia – each of which is equivalent to Arabia as a population centre. The single group is enough for our purposes, however, as the history of the Hamites is not very exciting and requires little detail. Even more is this true of the Finns, whose role is one of passive contraction. We are left with one expansionist sub-race, the Indo-European, and two minor ones that get largely overrun by Indo-Europeans in early historical times, the West Mediterranean and the Caucasian.

The current structure and past evolution of the major sub-races is not a very controversial matter,

but the status of the West Mediterranean and Caucasian groups is much less certain. The surviving representative of the West Mediterranean group is Basque, now restricted to the Western Pyrenees. Place-name and blood-group evidence indicates that once the Basques occupied not only all of Spain, but also France at least as far north and east as the Loire and Rhône. This distribution corresponds with that of the historical people known as Iberians and, although we cannot read the few inscriptions that the Iberians have left us, they are usually, and reasonably, taken as being ancestral to the Basques.

From the Rhône it is not far to Tuscany, which was inhabited in the first millennium B.C. by the only other European people who can be considered candidates for membership of the West Mediterranean group, the Etruscans. We can understand the sense of Etruscan inscriptions but cannot analyse the structure of the language sufficiently well to establish its relationships; all that seems certain is that it is not Indo-European. This purely negative distinction is the sole justification for placing Basque and Etruscan together, and the group only exists in opposition to Indo-European.

The Caucasian group survives in a number of languages spoken in the Transcaucasian region of the U.S.S.R. Georgian is the best known; some of the minor ones have been little investigated, but the group is commonly regarded as a genetically sound one. The language of the ancient Kingdom of Van certainly and of the Hattites, Kassites and Elamites very probably form part of this group. As for the Sumerians, they were neither Semitic nor Indo-European and, pending further research, membership of the Caucasian group is a reasonable postulate on negative grounds. Even without the Sumerians this gives us a minimum distribution for the original Caucasians stretching from the east of Anatolia to the western edge of the Iranian plateau.

Both Basque and Georgian are linguistically

agglutinative (that is, use prefixes and suffixes for declension as opposed to inflectional languages like Indo-European, where the changes are internal). Is there a possibility of linking the two into a single Mediterranean–Caucasian group, fragmented geographically in the late prehistoric period by the arrival of the Indo-Europeans at various points on the northern shore of the Mediterranean? The simple answer is that we don't know. However, few people are content to let the problem alone pending the appearance of fresh evidence because it relates to the classic enigma of ancient history, the origin of the Etruscans.

The Etruscans claimed that they were immigrants to Tuscany, having come from Western Anatolia – presumably around 900 B.C. Modern opinion is divided about this claim, the believers on the whole predominating. Their arguments are based on:

1. The Etruscan tradition.

2. The higher cultural level of the Etruscans as against the Italics in the second quarter of the last millennium B.C.

3. Various cultural features in Iron Age Etruria that are reminiscent of the Aegean–Anatolian region.

4. The presence of apparently Etruscan inscriptions on the Aegean island of Lemnos in sufficient number to indicate that this was the language of the inhabitants.

The first three of these are, as evidence, largely worthless. The Etruscans claimed to be Lydians but Lydian is an Indo-European language and even in antiquity it was noted that

1. Statements of the class 'Celtic is a linguistic not a racial grouping' are still made with unfortunate frequency and emphasis. In the strict sense this is true for Celtic is a sub-racial grouping but, in its implication that the Celts were never a geographically and socially definable population, it is certainly wrong.

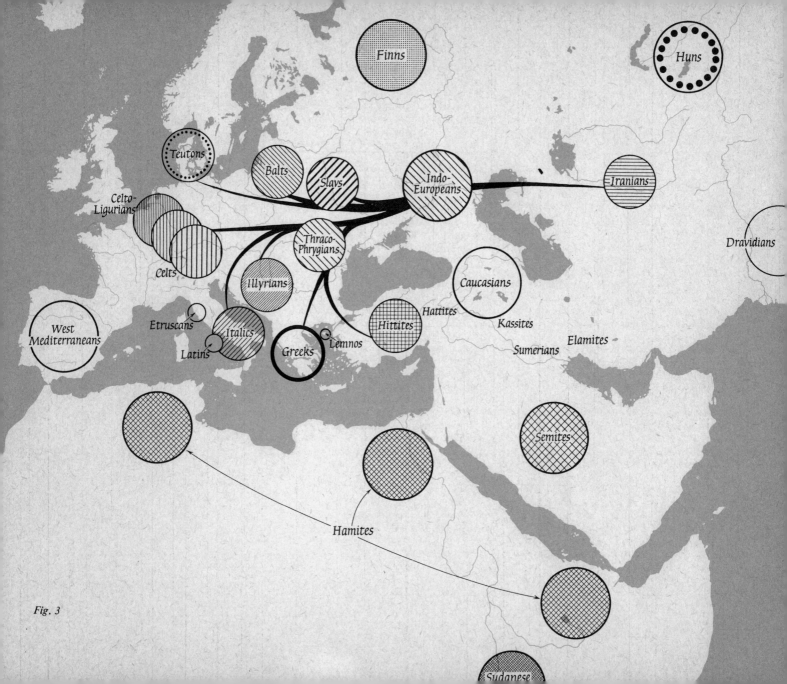

Finns

Huns

Teutons

Balts

Slavs

Indo-
Europeans

Iranians

Celto-
Ligurians

Thraco-
Phrygians

Dravidians

Celts

Illyrians

Caucasians

Etruscans

Hattites

Hittites

West
Mediterraneans

Italics

Kassites

Latins

Greeks

Lemnos

Sumerians

Elamites

Hamites

Semites

Fig. 3

Sudanese

Etruscan and Lydian were quite dissimilar. The legend of their origin is to be taken no more seriously than the Romans' tale of their Trojan descent, being only one of many myths synthesized to create a respectable past for the newer Mediterranean communities. It is true that the Phoenicians emigrated a comparable distance at a comparable time but their homeland and their motivation were never lost sight of; neither were clear to the ancients in the Etruscan case and both are a complete mystery to us. The higher cultural level and the signs of Aegean contact are merely consequences of trade with the Greeks whose interest in Italy was focused on Tuscany by the iron and copper deposits of Elba and Etruria.

The last piece of evidence – the Lemnian inscriptions – is more difficult to evaluate. When a language is only very poorly understood, not too much weight can be given to such claims (it used to be said, before Ventris deciphered the script, that the only thing known for sure about Linear B was that it was not Greek), but assuming that there is a genuine similarity of language it will be seen that a pre-Greek language in the Aegean could be related to Etruscan without being ancestral to it: it could merely be another survivor of the West Mediterranean–Caucasian group hypothesized above, As evidence it does not weight one side or the other in the controversy on Etruscan origins.

The migration theory seems to me inherently improbable and it would require much stronger evidence than has yet been advanced to compel my belief. Moreover, it is a hypothesis in retreat and has been for a century. Pieces of evidence that were advanced in the past (for example, supposed linguistic similarities between Etruscan and Lydian) have been disproved and the expectations raised by its predictions (that the language of Linear B would turn out to be 'Etruscoid') have been disappointed. The pre-Greek Aegean languages are now thought to be related to Hittite. But the one sure thing is that, pending a

full decipherment of Etruscan, further controversy is sterile.

Distinctive shadings are used on the maps to differentiate the various sub-races. The Hamites and Semites are cross-hatched, the mesh being closer in the Hamitic case: in the valley of the White Nile an even closer mesh is used to mark the Sudanic-speaking peoples who represent the cline between Hamite and Negro. The Finns are stippled; the Caucasians and Georgians are unshaded, a choice that has the advantage of leaving their often very insecurely determined boundaries indefinite. The Indo-Europeans are originally diagonally lined; then as they expand and the various communities within the sub-race differentiate, new shadings are introduced for each. The process is diagrammatically illustrated in Fig. 3. The shadings are valid for the whole atlas.[1] It will be seen that two Indo-European peoples – the Latins and the Greeks – are not shaded at all but given a simple boundary. This is done entirely for pictorial reasons and does not imply that there is anything non-Indo-European about them or that they are close relatives within the Indo-European group. It would overweight the maps to shade the large areas involved, and in the Greek case a shading suitable for the Macedonian empire in its heyday would hardly do for the littoral distribution of the colonizing period. In the case of the Greeks the use of a boundary conflicts with another system that is otherwise used consistently in the political series of maps: only organized states have an outline. In the Greek case the line marks the boundary of the Greek people and the extent of the Greek world but does not imply any political cohesion.

In a sub-racial sense the atlas might be said to have the expansion and differentiation of the Indo-Europeans as its theme. In this context, however, it must be remembered that in the first half of the second millennium B.C. there was a two-pronged migration that carried a significant proportion of the Iranian people out of the area

shown on the base map. Starting from Transoxiana, one group of Iranians spread across Central Asia, becoming the basal population of the steppe, an environment they were the first to master: another group moved south and invaded India, conquering first the Indus and then the Ganges valleys. It was from the Iranians of Central Asia that the Huns, Turks and Mongols – the models of the nomad in medieval times – originally learnt the specialized form of pastoralism that became their hallmark. In the classical period Central Asia was dominated by Iranian peoples, and it was only towards its end that they began to yield to the Altaians – the sub-race consisting of the Turks and Mongols. (The Huns belonged to one or other of these two peoples, but the absence of adequate linguistic remains make it impossible to say which.) The migration of the Yue-Chi into the base map area, mentioned above, was in fact a reflux movement, the return of an Iranian people to their ancestral homeland as a result of defeat at the hands of the Huns. A century later a group of Hunnish tribes followed them; this was the first and only time Altaian peoples appeared in the west during the period covered by this book. They are distinguished by a border of circles.

In the introduction to the medieval companion to this atlas there is a short passage warning the reader not to place too much trust in historical maps; every historical statement is an act of selection and a map can be grossly misleading in emphasis. The warning is worth repeating here and, as far as the earlier maps which deal with

1. They are also valid for the *Medieval Atlas* except that 1) the sole medieval survivor of the Thraco-Phrygian peoples, the Armenians, are therein shaded as Iranian, and 2) the Hittites having long since vanished, their shading is used for the Russians when the time comes to distinguish them from the rest of the Slavs.

prehistory are concerned, needs underlining. For with prehistory we enter a world of few facts and much guesswork, a world moreover which is ruled by the archaeologists. This is worrying; while field-work has become an exact and exacting craft, archaeological discussion is as often an indulgence as a discipline; where they might exchange hypotheses archaeologists are apt to demand adherence and to hurl polemics or even charges of corruption.

Archaeological argument gets more heated in tone and uncertain in structure the further removed the subject matter is from older, calmer studies; hence for the historical period the situation is good, the information recovered being subjected to a scholarly routine evolved to integrate it with existing knowledge. That a distribution can be given for the Roman legions for Maps A.D. 14–230 of this atlas, for example, is thanks to a hundred years of painstaking unspectacular archaeological and epigraphical work, equally carefully interpreted. In prehistory on the other hand the archaeologist has been on his own; he has not only discovered the unlettered past, he has read it out for all to hear; he has made pronouncements in a dozen fields from metallurgy to sociology; he has had flights of fancy and fits of bad temper; he has been generally unlovely.

The great pioneers who led archaeology beyond the frontiers of recorded history invested very considerable personal fortunes in their chosen sites; striding confidently round their estates they would label an unexpected pot as an import and expect obedience. The habit of omnipotence spread to lesser men in colder climates; amazingly it proved possible to give blow-by-blow accounts of prehistoric battles and, in a more tender mood, tell how Woman shaped the First Pot. Archaeology was acclaimed as the science of rubbish and as fast as the rubbish was dug up it was written down.

Inevitably poetic licence bred a puritan reaction within the profession, the puritans gained power and there was a ruthless clean-up. Not only was speculation condemned, intellectual activity of any sort came to be frowned upon. The new style archaeologist showed signs of distress if he uncovered an object of beauty or value; salvation lay in the meticulous description of humbler finds. Classification was allowable; sub-classification was better; attempts at synthesis or interpretation met with stony silence. As a corrective, puritanism has certainly been valuable but as a permanent attitude it is unnecessarily limiting; the recovery of the human past is after all the only reason for digging up pots.

The unit of prehistorical discussion is the culture, characterized by a defined range of artefacts. The culture may be named after a particularly rich or particularly well described site, after a unique artefact or after the area in which sites of the type occur most frequently. For each such culture we can plot a geographical distribution and by radiocarbon dating obtain an estimate of its date and duration. It is then a simple task to draw up a series of prehistorical maps showing a sequence of cultures analogous to the sequence of peoples and states on historical maps.[1] It is also easy to add lines to show the limits of certain techniques such as farming or metalworking. But what about people? People move and how can we tell whether the displacement of one culture by another indicates an invasion or a change of fashion?

We are not so helpless in this matter as the puritans pretend. For example the *Danubian* culture, the earliest Neolithic culture of Central Europe, has a comparatively small area of contact with the old-established Neolithic communities of the Balkans which indicates that its originators were few; it undoubtedly represents a spread by these originators because the type of shifting agriculture they had evolved would rapidly disperse any population practising it. And the density of a Neolithic people being greater than that of a mesolithic one by a factor of at least ten, the ethnic contribution of the aborigines – even if they were absorbed rather than exterminated or expelled – must have been insignificant. And given that the *Danubians* were a genuine people and remained so until provincial differences began to appear among them a millennium after they had expanded across Central Europe, it is difficult to avoid the view that their movement created an Indo-European heartland which must be postulated for roughly this time and place on purely linguistic grounds. Therefore the *Danubian* culture represents the arrival and establishment of the Indo-Europeans in Central Europe.

The main objection to this type of hypothesis is that it is untestable; it may be the simplest explanation of the known facts but, events being often complex and redundant, it does not necessarily follow that it is the right one. It is true that at the moment we have no means of evaluating such hypotheses except in terms of simplicity; the attempts to establish definite rates of change for languages (lexicostatistics) and to determine the genotypes of ancient peoples from their skeletal remains (palaeoserology) have so far proved unsuccessful; but though the time is not yet it is obviously coming. It is perfectly

1. The names of archaeologically defined cultures and peoples are italicized in the text and written in sans serif script on the maps. The boundaries given for them need not be taken too seriously as there is always a considerable overlap between cultures which it is impossible to show on maps of small scale. The dating of cultures is probably accurate to within ten per cent of the date B.C.; this compares with about five per cent for the early historical period and a margin of error of only a year or so from Assyrian times in the eastern Mediterranean and from the Punic Wars in the west.

In many books spuriously exact dates are given for the early historical period. These derive either from fragmentary annals which supply an accurate relative chronology but whose absolute date is arguable, or from the calculations of ancient scholars whose genealogical method was incapable of yielding precise results. I have rounded dates of the first class to the nearest five or ten and indicated that those of the second class are simply traditional.

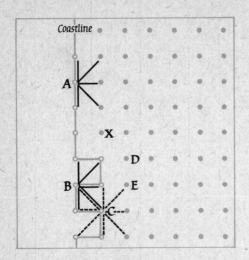

*Fig. 4.* Theoretical relationships between littoral and inland communities, with both evenly distributed. On the straight stretch of coast A relates to three inland and two littoral communities; on the indented stretch B's connexions are exclusively littoral, while C's relationships with littoral communities outnumber its inland connexions by five to three. B and C lie within a littoral ecosphere whereas A does not. If the upper indentation extended inland one unit further, to D–E, the inland community at X would be incorporated in the littoral zone, though out of sight of the sea.

respectable to make predictions outside the area of the currently ascertainable and as this atlas is intended to present the evolution of European and Near Eastern society I have been as free with such hypotheses as is necessary to make a connected story. The text contains only the occasional warning about this, for it should be obvious that a prehistory in ethnic terms is by definition hypothetical.

History being a branch of the biological sciences its ultimate expression must be mathematical. As yet we have only just groped our way from narrative history with its colour and crises,

its national heroes and nations personified, to the era of economics, of steel production figures and graphs of agricultural prices. The classical world is not comprehensible in the new terminology; it usually returns a 'no' or 'don't know' to the economic questionnaire; and the study of ancient history is probably going to continue unchanged until history as a whole passes into the next stage. This is foreshadowed by the increasing interest in sociology, and though currently most sociological work yields only platitudes expressed in jargon, in time a language will undoubtedly be created for the description of human societies and statements concerning their cohesion.

The time is not yet, but it is perhaps worth considering some problems of ancient history in a more objective way than is as yet current. Take the Greeks. We have spoken of ecospheres for races and sub-races and defined their boundaries as discontinuities in the environment which isolate the population to either side. The littoral distribution of the Greeks prior to the fourth century B.C. is a particularly subtle example of an ecosphere, for there is no physical barrier between a coastal people and the inhabitants of the hinterland, only a social barrier due to their differing ways of life.

What are the factors that govern the evolution and spread of littoral cultures? A reasonable model of the ecological situation would postulate an even distribution of communities with purely local relationships. Figure 4 shows that on a straight stretch of coast, as in the upper part of the diagram, the relationships between sea-shore communities are weaker than their relationships with inland communities by a factor of three to two; whereas in the lower half, where the coastline is indented, not only is the number of sea-shore communities greatly increased but the relationships between them frequently outnumber their other relationships and are sometimes exclusive. This theoretical analysis suggests that it is redundant coastline that generates the social co-

hesion necessary for the transformation of a series of littoral communities into an ecosphere. Figure 5 attempts to test this hypothesis by measuring the irregularity of the Mediterranean coast. It was constructed by placing a transparency ruled with a grid over the whole area and colouring red each square containing a segment of coastline. A second, identical transparency and grid was then superimposed on the first, and on this, every square which had a majority of red squares among its eight immediate neighbours was coloured blue. Remove the first transparency and you have Fig. 5. This purely geographical manipulation outlines a number of areas, of which much the largest includes the Greek Peninsula, the Aegean Islands and Ionia with an extension north-eastward to the Bosporus. The areas of the same type which lie closest to this primary zone are the South Russian coast, Cyprus, the heel of Italy, Sicily and Dalmatia. The Greeks orginally occupied peninsular Greece and the Aegean Islands, then Cyprus; at the beginning of the last millennium B.C. they occupied Ionia and from the eighth century on colonized the Bosporus region, the mouths of the great Russian rivers, the Southern Crimea and Cimmerian Bosporus, the heel and toe of Italy, Campania and Sicily. Two areas indicated by the theoretical analysis – Dalmatia and the Northern Crimea – were never occupied by the Greeks. Otherwise the fit is surprisingly good.

The remaining areas picked out by this technique lie mostly in the western Mediterranean where, during the Greek colonizing period, the Carthaginians were the dominant sea-power. Once again the areas indicated by the geographical analysis correspond reasonably well to the early centres of Carthaginian activity. Groups of less than four squares need not be taken too seriously, though the picking out of Massilia is interesting and it is perhaps worth noting that the only points indicated as being significant to a littoral culture in the Levant and in Egypt approximately coincide with the points where the Greeks at an early stage attempted to establish themselves, and with the two major centres of Hellenistic power, Antioch and Alexandria. However, at this point the argument begins to get a little specious; so much has happened in history and so much of it is due to the Greeks that it would be possible to justify squares chosen purely on a random basis.

Another objection that might be raised to this thesis is that it fails to pick out the pioneer seafarers of the Mediterranean world, the Phoenicians. However, the definition of a littoral ecosphere is not concerned with seagoing activity *per se* but with the relationship, or rather lack of it, between the coastal communities and those inland, and whereas both the Greeks and the Carthaginians differed in culture and language from the peoples who occupied their hinterlands the Phoenicians were essentially similar to the inhabitants of Syria and the Lebanon.

As befits the largest of the Mediterranean littoral ecospheres the central Greek zone has proved much the most stable. In fact the outline of the ethnically Greek area underwent its most significant alteration comparatively recently with the expulsion of the Ionian Greeks by the Turks in 1922.

There is, of course, a conflict of interest between continental and littoral peoples but this does not become overt until the continental communities become organized into a centralized state. It is only then that the national aspirations are formulated and that there is a drive for 'natural frontiers', by which is simply meant geographically easily recognizable features such as rivers, mountain ranges or, best of all, the sea. The concept of the natural frontier is much easier to grasp than the concept of an ecosphere boundary and once attained is considerably easier to administer. It is not surprising that the elimination of any littoral blemish on its sovereignty is among the first objectives which the new state sets itself.[1]

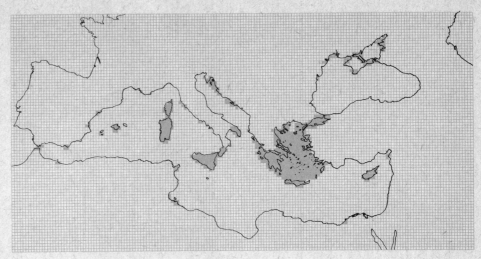

*Fig. 5.* Littoral zones in the Mediterranean. For explanation see text.

It is usual to attempt to assess the progress of national organization in administrative terms but degrees of central control are difficult to quantify and it is worthwhile looking at the pattern of settlement again in this context. In an unorganized group of communities the size of the individual community will not vary much from the mean of the series; in a centralized state the capital will attract extra population to serve the needs of the administrators. Accordingly, the metropolis of the centralized state can be expected to have a size – in archaeological terms this means an area – several times greater than the largest of the ordinary communities that have been incorporated in it.[2] In the Greek case the relationship between the Ionians and the peoples of the Anatolian hinterland was tranquil in the Phrygian period but deteriorated steadily after the establishment of the Lydian monarchy; archaeological evidence is as yet only slight but it looks as though Gordium, the capital of the Phrygian kingdom,

covered an area of only about twenty-five acres, which puts it well within the normal range of

1. Many wars owe their origin to this type of conflict. A river valley is itself an ecosphere and its division is usually unnatural in social terms; for example, both banks of the Rhine have had a German population ever since Roman times, but to the French the line of the river seems a natural frontier. The eastern Alps are another homogeneously German zone; the southern boundary on an ecological analysis lies along the foothills whereas the natural frontier in Italian eyes is the watershed.

2. The built-up area can only be assessed directly in the relatively few instances where excavation has been near complete. In the vast majority of cases for which figures are quoted these refer to the area enclosed by the walls. The line of the walls is often distorted by the topography and in the individual case the figure may be very misleading. Also, fashions in fortification change – the Greeks favoured extensive perimeters, the Romans a minimal circuit – so comparisons between areas enclosed at different dates can be meaningless. However, the assumption that the area fortified and the population contained relate in an approximate way is reasonable in itself and can to some extent be validated for the Roman period by a comparison between size and administrative rank (see Fig. 6).

11

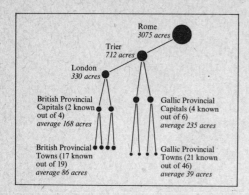

*Fig. 6.* Administrative hierarchy and walled area of cities in the British and Gallic provinces of the Roman Empire. The walls are mostly third century; the higher average for the provincial towns in Britain as against France is probably only a reflection of their earlier date (beginning as opposed to end of the third century) for throughout the Roman period circuits grew tighter. The provincial divisions are those of the fourth century.

early Iron Age communities, while Sardes, the Lydian metropolis, was at least ten times as big as this. This accords well with the judgement of historians that the Lydian state was organized in a much more significant way than the Phrygian.

The statement that it is the administrative apparatus that swells the capital and gives it its unique size is, of course, a gross over-simplification only true of an imposed metropolis such as Roman London. Britain throughout the first millennium A.D. was a patchwork of county-sized communities, and, though the Romans saw the island as a single province, the inhabitants did not. Consequently, the metropolis disappeared with the end of Roman rule. The growth of national consciousness was a slow process; London did not regain exceptional status till the eleventh century, and only after the Norman Conquest were both capital and kingdom estab-

lished as permanent entities. There is more to a state than its administration, more to a kingdom than a court and more to a capital than the presence of these institutions; the growth of the metropolis is itself part of the social change involved in the recognition of unity.

In absolute terms the size of a metropolis must be governed by such factors as the area of its influence, the shape, communication lines and population density of this area, and the general social, economic and technological level of the period concerned. The relationships are obviously complex and beyond exact expression in the current state of our understanding but, even if its effect is modified by the other factors, the presence of area of influence in the hypothetical equation is interesting. For the equation concerns the stable condition and historical processes are dynamic; the metropolis that is without a balancing area of influence will be expansionist; the area that contains too many cities of metropolitan rank will be torn by continuous and apparently inexplicable warfare. Athens and Greece in the classical period, Venice and Northern Italy in later medieval times, are examples that fit these patterns which, if they are accepted as having general validity, suggest that the question a historian should ask himself is not 'Why did Athens gain an empire?' but 'Why in the pre-Imperial phase did the population of Athens increase so rapidly?' Perhaps our understanding of the problem will be greater when we have discovered why human beings prefer urban to rural poverty, why big cities have an attraction beyond any economic advantage, why sponsored emigration schemes always fail to solve the problem of an unemployed urban proletariat. Perhaps the key to the mystery of Rome's apparently inexorable rise to greatness will be found in the slums of Calcutta.

With the exception of mountains the geographical features named in this book are shown on the

index map at the back; mountains deserve a special note because of their obvious importance as physical barriers. The simplest and most convincing examples of mountain frontiers are the Pyrenees and Alps, which partially seal off the Iberian and Italian peninsulas. Minor ranges isolate Bohemia; the Carpathians give Hungary a natural border in the east. Some ranges of greater height are of less significance; the Atlas merely parallels the edge of the Sahara, and the Arabian ranges are of little importance because the dominant environmental factor is the desert. But in Asia the mountains have made history and as their names are less familiar a brief survey is perhaps in order (see Fig. 7). Starting in Turkey we have the Anatolian plateau, then the Armenian knot; eastward from this is the Iranian plateau whose western edge – the Zagros range – overlooks Mesopotamia. Most of the eastern half of the Iranian plateau is occupied by the Great Salt Desert (Dasht-i-Lut). Now take the perpendicular from the centre of the Iranian plateau to the upper border of the map and to the left of the mountain zone of central Asia. (The compass bearing is north–east because the north–south line cuts obliquely across the top right-hand corner of the map.) The sequence of features is 1) the northern edge of the Iranian plateau; 2) the Kara Kum (Black Desert); 3) the Oxus river; 4) the Kizil Kum (Red Desert); 5) the Jaxartes river; 6) another desert zone; and 7) Lake Balkhash, the L-shaped sump of the Ili river. From there another 1,700 miles on the same course (which now becomes eastward) would take us to Peking. This is roughly the same as the distance back from Lake Balkhash to the Black Sea.

Now go back to the Iranian plateau and make the crossing from the right-hand end to the middle Indus; this is the Bolan Pass in the Sulaiman range, the pass used by the Saka invaders of India in the first century B.C. Most of the invasions of the sub-continent have taken place by the next one up, the Khyber Pass between

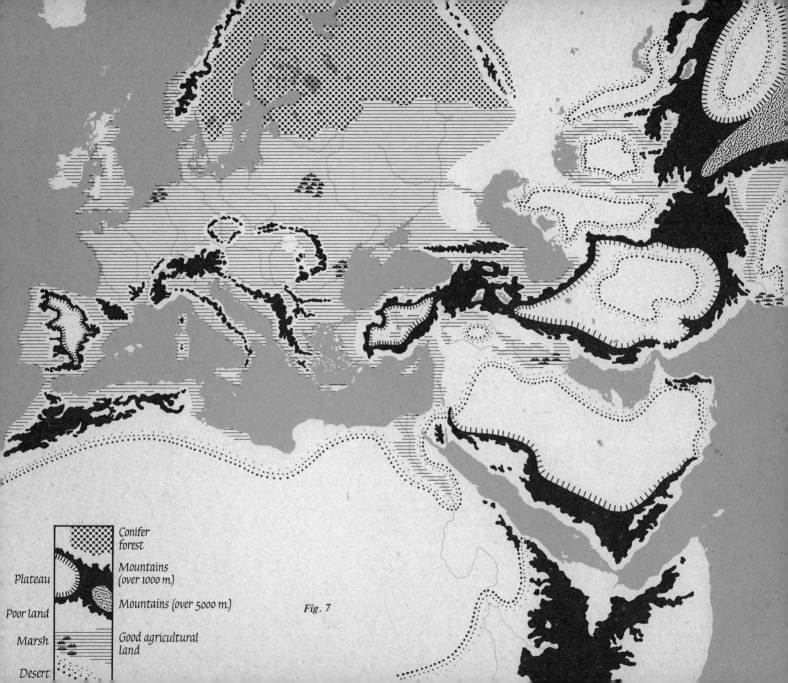

Conifer
forest

Mountains
(over 1000 m.)

Plateau

Mountains (over 5000 m.)

Poor land

Fig. 7

Marsh

Good agricultural
land

Desert

the Upper Oxus valley (the province of Bactria) and the valley of the Kabul tributary of the upper Indus. Kabul town is situated mid-way between Oxus and Indus at the tip of the main, 5,000 metre, Central Asian Massif. The tip is the Hindu Kush, the Indian edge the Himalayas and the other edge facing the oval plateau in the top right-hand corner, the Kun Lun range. The Himalayan and Kun Lun edges diverge, the space between them becoming further east the Tibetan plateau (not shown). The oval plateau of which the Kun Lun range forms the right-hand edge is the Tarim Basin; it can be entered either from Bactria or from the upper Jaxartes valley (Ferghana), by passes over the Pamirs. The Pamir–Tarim Basin route is an alternative road to China and was in fact the one taken by the ancient silk route. The left-hand border of the Tarim basin is formed by the Tien Shan (Celestial Mountains); the lower (western) Tien Shan form the current border between Russian and Chinese Turkestan; the latter is also known as Sinkiang, a term sometimes used to mean the Tarim Basin, though it includes a rather larger area.

Starting from the Tien Shan and coming down again towards the Iranian plateau but this time sticking to the mountain zone we have 1) the Pamir knot 2) the Hindu Kush 3) the Afghanistanian knot and finally 4) the Sulaiman range, the eastern border of the Iranian plateau.

The coastline given on this map and on all except the first three maps of the following series is the modern one. On the theory that the deposition of the silt borne by the Tigris and Euphrates would result in a gradual advance of the coast, many historical atlases show the Persian Gulf during the millennia preceding the Christian era extending over the lower part of Iraq. Current geographical opinion rejects this view; the deposition of silt is considered to be balanced by subsidence due to the additional weight. In the absence of evidence to the contrary all river deltas, including the Nile and the Indus, are here regarded as stable in this dynamic sense. The only changes shown in the coastline are those associated with the last ice age, which caused a general lowering of the sea level and certain local distortions due to the icecaps. The land actually covered by the icecap sank under the colossal weight imposed on it, while that just beyond its rim underwent a much smaller compensatory uplift. As the icecap retreated the terrain uncovered began to rise, but this recovery lagged so far behind the removal of the weight that the most depressed areas – Scotland and the middle region of the Baltic–have not completed the movement at the present time. When the Baltic became a sea it was consequently somewhat larger than at present, and conversely, although when the current world sea level was reached (c.5500 B.C.) 'North-Sea-Land' was submerged and the Channel formed, the delay in the subsidence of the rim allowed the Dogger Bank and some areas of the English and Dutch coasts, where a few fathoms are critical, to continue for a while as dry land.

This book does not pretend to scholarship; it has been compiled almost exclusively from secondary sources and that is an exhausting enough task in itself. Among those who have sustained my enthusiasm I am particularly grateful to Peter Fison with whom I have had many stimulating discussions; the text has benefited from his advice as greatly as I have from his friendship. I have also been much assisted by the encouragement of my brother Brian McEvedy, by the secretarial talent of Kate McKinnon Wood, Stephanie Thompson and Jean Paine and by the general and essential aid furnished by my wife.

14

# The Atlas

# 50,000 B.C.

The term 'ape-man', implying a half-way stage in the evolution of ape into man, can be fairly applied to the Australopithecines that lived in Africa between one and two million years ago. They were sufficiently bright to shape pebbles so as to give them a cutting edge, but lacked knowledge of fire. The Pithecanthropoids, whose remains are distributed across Europe, Africa, China and Indonesia and date to the period 750,000–250,000 B.C. are definitely, if primitively, human. They knew about fire, and their tools were standardized and skilfully wrought. No comparable advances can be associated with the appearance of *Homo sapiens* (perhaps 150,000 years ago), but there can be little doubt that he was quicker thinking than the primitives and demonstrated his superiority by hunting them down. If the evidence for man's descent is scanty, we can thank our ancestors who probably ate most of it.

During the Pleistocene period – the geological term for the last 2,000,000 years – the earth's climate underwent slow fluctuations, passing from warm to cold and back again.[1] During the extremes of the cold phases, the glaciers normally confined to high mountain ranges expanded and coalesced until an ice sheet hundreds of feet thick covered much of northern Europe as Greenland is covered today. Further south, in the Himalayas and Alps, although the glaciers grew there was enough summer left to prevent them extending over the lowlands, and the climate remained moderate. South of the glaciated zone, rainfall tended to be heavy because of the interaction of warm southern air and air from the ice-chilled north, and this heavier rainfall supported a fairly vigorous flora and fauna in the Sahara and other areas that are now desert. Combined with the diminished evaporation rate, it also caused a general rise in lake levels which was accentuated in the case of the Aral and Caspian both by the flow of meltwater

16

from the icecaps in their drainage area and by the reversal of flow in the north Russian rivers, whose normal outlet was dammed by the ice. The end result was a single Aral-Caspian system discharging its surplus into the Black Sea. As the locking-up of vast quantities of water in the ice-sheets produced a fall in sea level greater than the depth of the Dardanelles, the Black Sea too became a fresh-water lake.

It was probably in the last interglacial that Man (*Homo sapiens*) came into his own. During the early phase (60–50,000 B.C.) of the final (Wurm) glaciation, Europe and the Near East were inhabited, so far as we know exclusively, by a now extinct race of *Homo sapiens*, the Neanderthal.[2] Beyond the fact that he was a cave dweller and a hunter, little is known of his habits; remains of bear cult ceremonies have been discovered and he sometimes buried his dead in a manner that implies a belief in life after death.

The map shows the icecaps of the last ice age at the time of their greatest extent (Wurm, first peak); the sea is correspondingly at its lowest level, some one hundred metres below the present shore-line. Sites where Neanderthal skeletal material has been found are marked with a cross. Not all the finds date from the first Wurm maximum, but none goes back much beyond the beginning of this cold phase, and Neanderthal man is known to have become extinct early on its waning. His remains, and the *Mousterian*-style flint tools that are his characteristic handiwork, have been found at points scattered widely across the area shown but, as neither occur outside it, the Europe–Near East area, in its cold phase, can be regarded as the Neanderthalers' ecosphere.[3] The few European skeletal fragments known from the pre-Wurm interglacial period are either similar to those of modern men or else mildly neanderthaloid, the supposition being that the Neanderthal trend did not become dominant until the ice age isolated Europe from Asia and Africa.

1. There is still no very convincing explanation of the instability of climate in Pleistocene times. It is probably related to a steady lowering of sea level following the changes produced by continental drift in the capacity of the ocean basins. This gradual fall is to be distinguished from the changes caused by the glaciations themselves.

2. The typical Neanderthal skull is distinguishable at a glance from that of modern man. This distinction, which cannot be made in the case of modern races, caused anthropologists to exclude him from the species *sapiens*, and the gap was further widened by imaginative reconstructions, the shaggy animal peering out of the favoured versions seeming barely anthropoid. We have, of course, no information as to how hairy the Neanderthaler was and though his brow was certainly both massive and receding, his brain was every bit as big as ours and his posture as upright. Nowadays he is often labelled *Homo sapiens* (Neanderthal variant) rather than *Homo neanderthalensis* and it is considered that, suitably clothed, a Neanderthaler could pass unremarked along the banks of the Liffey.

3. *Mousterian* implements – and a possibly Neanderthal jaw – have been reported from South Africa.

x  Skeletal evidence of Neanderthal man

# 50,000 B.C.

# 8500 B.C.

Modern man (*Homo sapiens sapiens*) appeared in Europe soon after the Wurm icecap had begun its slow irregular shrinkage, but for many millennia the climate was to continue sub-Arctic with appropriate fauna – mammoth, woolly rhino, bear, bison and reindeer – and his way of life, that of a cave-dwelling hunter, was essentially the same as the Neanderthalers'. The upper palaeolithic[1] style of artefact he brought with him is, however, an advance on the Neanderthalers' *Mousterian*, showing greater variety and specialization of tool; it is also more widely spread, being found across the breadth of Europe and Asia. Within the upper palaeolithic, the archaeologist recognizes the sequence: *Châtelperronian, Aurignacian, Gravettian*, which last continues to the tenth millennium in Eastern Europe, the Near East and North Africa, but is replaced in Western Europe as early as the fifteenth millennium by the *Magdalenian*. The *Magdalenian*, an interesting example of complete dependence on a single biological source, the reindeer, owes its fame to the cave paintings of south-west France and northern Spain. Representative art was perhaps originally stimulated by theories of sympathetic magic, the artist believing that he gained control over an object or situation depicted. The earliest surviving examples, dated to the *Aurignacian*, tend to be diagrammatic, but *Magdalenian* works show a confident naturalism. Besides its considerable aesthetic value, upper palaeolithic art conveys a certain amount of archaeological information: figures carrying bows and arrows confirm the early invention of this weapon, and stone penises and Venuses suggest religious practices of appealing simplicity.

There is little to be gained from discussing the racial varieties of upper palaeolithic man. In the nineteenth century every skeleton discovered was minutely described and each became the type of a new race. When the number of discoveries reached

double figures, the classification broke down under its own weight. It is now realized that the range of variation in any population renders such exact description of the individual pointless, the more so in the case of upper palaeolithic man because the variation in his case was probably particularly wide. The isolation of family-size groups favours the exaggeration of characteristics by inbreeding, a state of affairs well exemplified in gorillas whose skulls are often startlingly different from one another.

The upper palaeolithic period came to an end during the ninth millennium B.C. when there was a rapid, though largely transitory, improvement in the climate (the Allerod oscillation), and a more permanent change in the flora and fauna of Europe. Therafter the reindeer and the upper palaeolithic tradition only survived near the diminishing icecap[2] (the *Ahrensburg-Lyngby* culture), and the majority of the inhabitants of Europe passed into a new cultural phase, the mesolithic (middle stone age). The mesolithic world is sometimes called impoverished because it lacked the art of the upper palaeolithic and the glamour of the bison chase. But though the largest quarry available were deer and oxen, and mesolithic man, to make ends meet, spent most of his time hunting the inglorious snail and the frankly sessile nut, his tools show considerable progress: wooden saws with rows of small geometrically chipped flints for teeth for example.[3]

Man's success is due to lack of specialization, to being able to change habit and diet when occasion demands. The creatures that exactly fitted the ice age ecology became extinct on its passing while man hung on, at first precariously, then, as he gradually explored the possibilities of the new environment, with increasing confidence. In the ninth millennium, the Iraqis of the upper Tigris valley and in the eighth, the Palestinians of the *Natufian* culture were supplementing their meagre fare with wild wheat. Flint sickles and mortars and pestles demonstrate no more than this and the

phrase 'incipient agriculture' applied to these cultures is oppressively teleological, but the planting of the crop, the final advance needed to carry man out of the mesolithic, food-gathering state and into the agriculture of the neolithic was in fact close at hand.

1. The palaeolithic (old stone age) is divided into lower and upper (old and recent considered stratigraphically) by the first peak of the Wurm glaciation. The *Mousterian* phase that marks the division is the middle palaeolithic.
2. As the sea level rose above the Bosporan shelf, salt water diffused into the Black Sea and killed the fresh-water life it contained. The decomposed remains of this ice-age population still poison the lower levels of the stagnant Black Sea which is devoid of life below 250 feet.
3. The boat was probably an invention of this period. The dog, which presumably was suffering from the disappearance of its prey in much the same way as man, first appears as a mesolithic camp-follower.

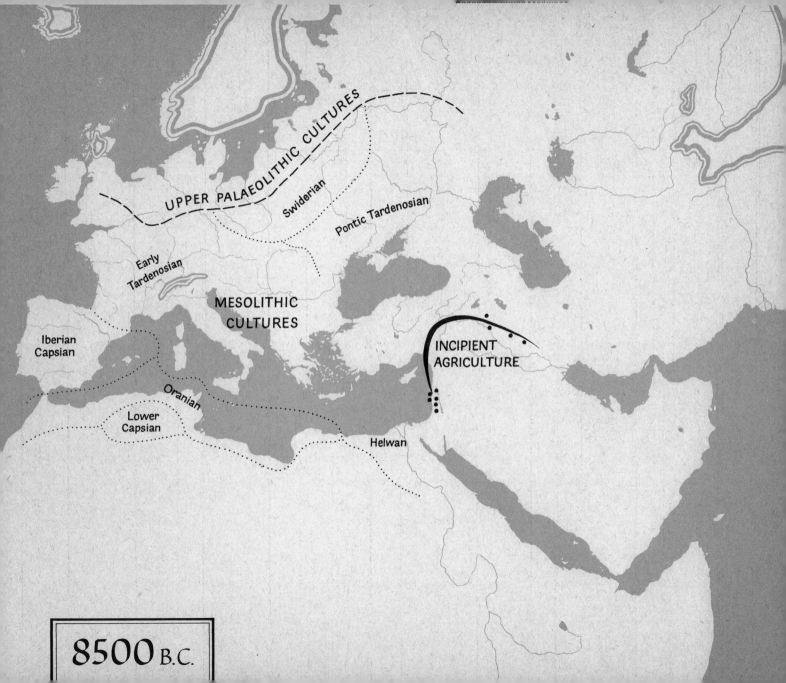

UPPER PALAEOLITHIC CULTURES

Swiderian

Pontic Tardenosian

Early
Tardenosian

MESOLITHIC
CULTURES

Iberian
Capsian

INCIPIENT
AGRICULTURE

Oranian

Lower
Capsian

Helwan

8500 B.C.

# 4500 B.C.

The transition from the mesolithic to the neolithic way of life is a turning-point in man's social and economic development comparable in importance to the industrial and scientific revolutions of the nineteenth and twentieth centuries. The contrast between a temporary mesolithic camp and a village of neolithic farmers is certainly striking enough to justify the term 'neolithic revolution', but just as modern technology makes its most dramatic appearance in backward countries, so the neolithic was at its most 'revolutionary' when, in its fully developed form, it spread beyond the Near-Eastern area where it had evolved into mesolithic Europe, Africa and Asia.

The innovations of the neolithic are many: the cultivation of wheat and barley, the domestication of goats, sheep, pigs and cattle, the use of fired pottery and of polished (as opposed to chipped) stone tools. It is to be expected that as more is learnt of the Near East during the critical period, which would appear to be the seventh millennium B.C., the picture of a revolutionary leap forward will be resolved into a series of slow and irregular advances in agriculture and artefacts. So far only one intermediate stage between the incipient agriculture of the eighth millennium and the fully evolved neolithic of the sixth has been at all adequately demonstrated. This is somewhat inelegantly called 'pre-pottery neolithic' because it satisfies all the social criteria but lacks the archaeologically most obvious artefact.[1] All of the dozen sites in the pre-pottery neolithic category so far discovered are within the fertile crescent – the 'incipient agriculture' region of the previous map; the best known is Jericho, a walled hamlet covering some ten acres whose inhabitants planted corn and kept goats. Apart from the fortification, which implies a level of social organization that was thought not to antedate the chalcolithic, the excavation of Jericho has provided a 'missing link' which falls easily into place within the Near Eastern evolutionary sequence.

By the sixth millennium the fully evolved neolithic had spread from the fertile crescent across Anatolia to the Balkans; at the same time the original neolithic communities of the Near East passed into the cultural phase known as chalcolithic, meaning copper- and stone-using.[2] Copper ores are noticeably coloured and can be smelted in the simple oven used for firing pottery; the discovery was, by itself, neither very remarkable nor very useful. Three major cultural zones are distinguished within the early Near-Eastern chalcolithic: the *Halafian* of Syria and northern Mesopotamia; the *Ghassulian* of Palestine; and the *Hacilar* of Anatolia. Chalcolithic pottery is characteristically painted; the technique apparently originated in Anatolia in neolithic times and spread out slightly in advance of chalcolithic technology.

Copper working remained confined to the Near East for 2,000 years after its discovery and during most of this period – the sixth and fifth millennia – the line marking the limit of neolithic techniques seems to have been equally static. But about 4500 there were two breakthroughs; one from Palestine to Egypt and the North African coast; and the other from the lower Danube region across Central Europe. In the case of the *Danubians* the reason for their rapid progress is easy to discern: they cleared their fields by burning the cover off virgin land and tilled them only for the few years in which yields remained high. On the move every few seasons, the *Danubians*, though neolithic, were more mobile than some of the mesolithic populations of the Baltic and Spanish coasts who established permanent communities wherever there was a sufficient supply of shellfish. The *Ertebolle* folk of Denmark and various other mesolithic groups on the eastern border of the neolithic zone learnt from the *Danubians* to make pottery and to polish their stone tools but kept at their food-gathering, a compromise called sub-neolithic. Elsewhere in Europe the scanty *Tardenosian* and *Maglemose* populations continued a purely mesolithic way of life.

The population build-up that the invention of agriculture entailed must have almost immediately created a stable sub-racial situation within the white race. No one has ever challenged the aboriginal status of the Semites in Arabia, and whether or not the related Hamites were neolithic immigrants or merely converts to agriculture (the latter is suggested for the Berbers by the continuity of stone-working techniques between the mesolithic and neolithic *Capsian* cultures) their dominance in North Africa from this time on is equally certain.[3] Similarly, the *Starcevo–Danubian* zone must surely have been Indo-European. Shadings are introduced for these three peoples at this point. We can also label the population of the Eastern Anatolia–Armenia–Western Iran region Caucasian; the mesolithic population of Western Europe as West Mediterranean; and of Northern Eurasia as Finnish. The boundaries between these peoples are, of course, disputable; the shaded areas may be regarded as minimal, it being quite reasonable to believe that the Indo-Europeans extended into the Baltic and Pontic sub-neolithic regions and the Aegean, that the Hamites already occupied Algeria and Morocco, and the Semites much of the fertile crescent.

The wedge protruding in from the right hand border of the map, which is a constant feature from now on, represents the Central Asian massif.

1. Using leather and basket-work containers (that have perished) and ground stone vessels (that survive), the seventh millennium villager no doubt managed happily enough; pots matter more to archaeologists than they do to people.
2. In the old classifications the Bronze Age followed directly on the Stone Age; cultures at the chalcolithic level of technology are sometimes still referred to as Early Bronze – for example in the Aegean. This is metallurgically incorrect; the term Copper Age is also unsatisfactory because stone remained the normal material for tools.
3. The same alternatives apply to the other Hamitic group, the Cushites of the Horn of Africa.

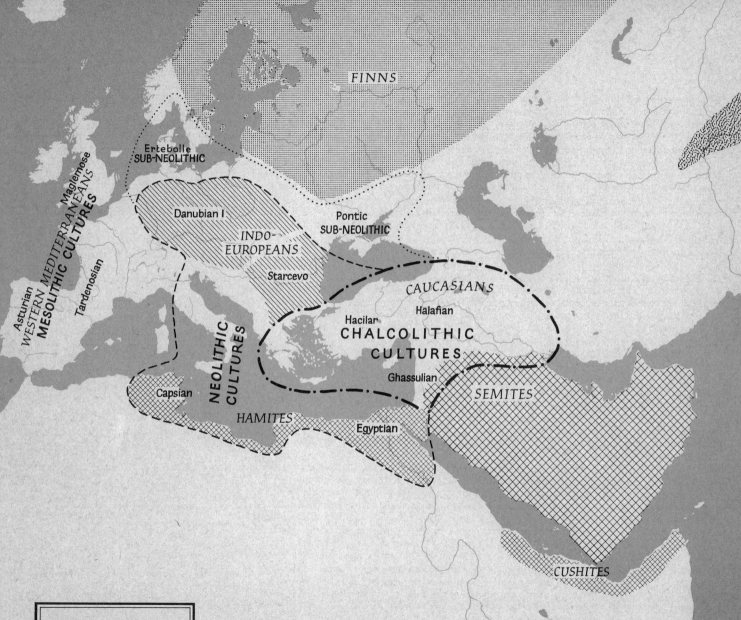

FINNS

Ertebolle
SUB-NEOLITHIC

Danubian I

INDO-
EUROPEANS

Pontic
SUB-NEOLITHIC

Starcevo

CAUCASIANS

Halafian

Hacilar

CHALCOLITHIC
CULTURES

Asturian
WESTERN MEDITERRANEAN
MESOLITHIC CULTURES

Maglemose

Tardenosian

NEOLITHIC
CULTURES

Capsian

HAMITES

Egyptian

Ghassulian

SEMITES

CUSHITES

4500 B.C.

# 2750 B.C.

Though neolithic agricultural techniques caused a quantum leap in population wherever they were applied, the rise was most marked where the soil was most fertile. Such an area was lower Mesopotamia, and at the end of the fourth millennium the population density there reached the point where villages grew into towns, initiating another quantum jump, this time in the sphere of social organization. The surplus of a single village is small and uncertain; only when the resources of many are pooled is there sufficient to support whole-time craftsmen. In this quantitative effect lies the qualitative difference between the homogeneous rural community of small-holders and the many professions of the town. Civilization is synonymous, in every sense, with urbanization, and both had now begun. Detailed consideration of the process and of the beginnings of trade and of literacy will be found two maps further on; this map is concerned only with the political and technological consequences.

The curve of Mesopotamian prosperity began to rise in the middle of the fourth millennium with the *Ubaid* culture which gradually spread from the south-eastern to the northern third of the fertile crescent. The *Ubaid* folk, though still villagers, could undertake sizeable projects, for they built the first temples known. These inhabitants of lower (down-river, southern) Mesopotamia identify themselves as Sumerians in the succeeding *Uruk* period (late fourth millennium), the golden age of Mesopotamian discovery. All knowledge gained archaeologically is indirect and uncertain to a greater or lesser degree, but the ascription to the *Uruk*–Sumerians of writing is as secure as can be. Two other triumphs, the invention of the wheel (at first exclusively a potter's instrument, but during the next, *Early Dynastic* phase, applied to vehicles) and the discovery of bronze,[1] must remain *sub judice*, for the present

22

evidence of primacy may be merely the result of the concentration of archeological endeavour in Mesopotamia.

By the twenty-eighth century writing had spread across the fertile crescent to Egypt, and south-eastward to the Elamites. Bronze working remained unknown in Egypt, for so long believed to be the site of man's emergence from barbarism, but now relegated to the technological margin. The Egyptians did, however, erect the first considerable kingdom:[2] in the opening years of the third millennium Menes, King of Upper (up-river or southern) Egypt, conquered the delta to become the first Pharaoh of the first dynasty. One man already ruled the Nile from the first cataract to the sea at a time when the independent town, ruled by a priest-king, was to be the political unit in Mesopotamia for another half millennium.

With Egyptians and Sumerians declaring themselves, we gain our first linguistic data. Sumerian records early identify the Semitic Akkadians as the dominant people in central Mesopotamia; they were probably also dominant in the north (later Assyria) though a basal Caucasian (*Subarian*) layer has been postulated for no very good reason. Outside Mesopotamia, there would be two main centres of Semitic population, one in Syria and Palestine, one in southern Arabia; an area is left clear in the centre of the shading of Arabia in this and succeeding maps to indicate the paucity of inhabitants in the desert region. The Elamites are the southernmost of the Caucasian peoples inhabiting the Zagros; Sumerian affiliations are unknown, but are certainly not Semitic.

In the mid fourth millennium the Western European zone attained the neolithic level; the cultures that resulted are regarded as related and as constituting a *Western* family that it is usual to consider in opposition to the elaborating *Danubian* complex.[3] The contrast between the two is emphasized less now than formerly; there are *Danubian* elements in the *Chassey*, *Cortaillod* and *Sabadell* cultures of France, while the *Windmill Hill* of Britain, traditionally regarded as typically *Western*, is now considered as at best a hybrid. This has obvious implications for the spread of the Indo-Europeans at the expense of the Western Mediterraneans.

To the east the Indo-Europeans must by this time have spread as far as Turkestan; in Africa the Cushites will have reached the upper Nile.

1. Bronze is an alloy of copper and tin, stronger yet easier to cast than pure copper.
2. They were also the first to use stone for building, starting with the step-pyramid of Zoser (Third Dynasty, twenty-seventh century).
3. The Central European variants of the *Danubian II* complex are too numerous to show on a map of this scale. They include the *Rossen* in the western sector, the *Lengyel* in the centre and east, and the *Bukk* and *Theiss* in the south.

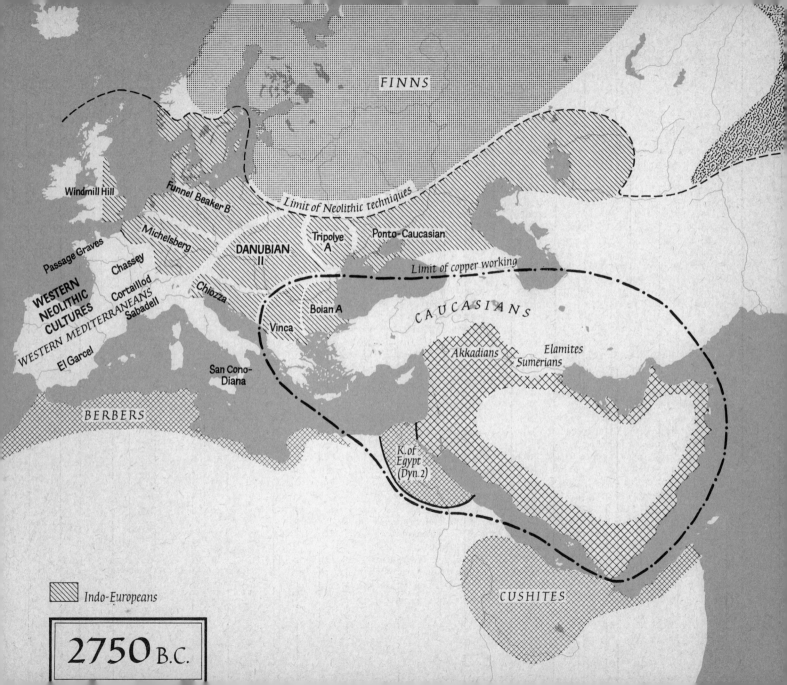

FINNS

Limit of Neolithic techniques

Windmill Hill

Funnel Beaker B

Michelsberg

Passage Graves

Chassey

WESTERN
NEOLITHIC
CULTURES

Cortaillod
Sabadell

Chiozza

WESTERN MEDITERRANEANS

El Garcel

DANUBIAN
II

Tripolye
A

Ponto-Caucasian

Limit of copper working

Vinca

Boian A

CAUCASIANS

Akkadians

Elamites
Sumerians

San Cono-
Diana

BERBERS

K. of
Egypt
(Dyn. 2)

CUSHITES

⬛ (hatched) Indo-Europeans

2750 B.C.

# 2250 B.C.

In the mid third millennium when the historical record opens,[1] the primacy for which the city states of Akkad and Sumer (central and southern Mesopotamia) contended, was held by Sumerian Lagash. It passed to the Semites of Kish in the twenty-fourth century, was briefly usurped by the Sumerian Lord of Umma and Erech, only to be regained for Kish by Sargon the Great in the opening years of the twenty-third century. Extending beyond the usual Mesopotamian horizon, Sargon added northern Mesopotamia and Elamite Susa to his Empire and his armies even penetrated into Syria and south-east Anatolia. But Sargonid glory was short-lived; around 2200 the Guti, one of the barbarian tribes of the Zagros that were to be the bane of the plainsmen, overran Akkad and the world's first empire disintegrated.

The Zagros tribes – Guti and Kassites – were Caucasians; the sites further east on the Iranian plateau show at this time a replacement of the hitherto characteristic painted pottery by a plain variety, a change that has been plausibly equated with the entry of the Iranians into their historical home. Mesopotamian records do not look far enough east to confirm or deny this. Another archaeologically deduced invasion, this time in central Anatolia, is generally accepted as marking the arrival of the Hittites. The simultaneous appearance from opposite directions of these two Indo-European peoples (who, as they can be named, are now given distinctive shadings) implies a minimal extent for the Indo-Europeans of the mid third millennium stretching in an arc across south Russia, from the Balkans to Turkestan.

The Hittite migration seems to have been only the central component in a trio of displacements starting with the *Usatova* movement from the Russian steppe into the Balkans and continued from eastern Anatolia into Syria and Palestine by the *Khirbet Kerak* folk. These last were members of the original population of Anatolia that is usually termed Hattite. Etymologically Hattite is synonymous with Hittite, meaning Anatolian irrespective of ethnic type; the Hittite (Indo-European) – Hattite (?Caucasian) distinction is, however, a necessary one.

While Mesopotamia reached a high-water mark under Sargon, Egypt was already declining from the exhausting magnificence of the pyramid-builders of the third and fourth dynasties. The defence problems of Egypt were small, a matter of overaweing the nomads of Libya and Sinai and the natives of Nubia upstream from the first cataract, and the Egyptian decline was a matter of gradual internal decay. The political unity of the country was lost around 2250, and thereafter separate dynasties ruled in Memphis (dynasty seven), Coptos and Abydos (eight) and Heracleopolis (nine and ten). This troubled period left no monuments, but through it the Egyptian tradition continued unbroken.

History's third literate civilization appeared in the Indus valley, to which it remained confined. It is called after either of the only two large towns discovered so far, Mohenjo-Daro and Harappa.

The spread of copper working up the Danube rendered the *Danubian III* complex of Central Europe[2] chalcolithic; with the adoption of primitive pit/comb pottery the Finno-Ugrian peoples passed from the mesolithic to the sub-neolithic. The full neolithic technology had spread across Asia to northern China by the mid third millennium. Metallurgically the Near East slipped back out of the Bronze Age during the second half of the third millennium with the exhaustion of the local tin deposits.

In the upper Nile valley a tighter version of the Hamitic shading marks the Sudanic zone, which is ethnically intermediate between Cushitic and Negro Africa.

1. For the twenty-sixth century, there is the legendary succession: Kish, Erech (the dynasty founded by the hero Gilgamesh) and Ur. The first Kishiote dynasty would seem to have been Sumerian, not Semitic. The sites of the towns mentioned are given on the next map.

2. Again exigencies of space prevent the display on the map of the three sub-cultures involved: the *Jordanovo* of Bohemia, the *Bodrogkereshtur* of the Theiss valley and the central *Baden* culture (which outlasts the other two).

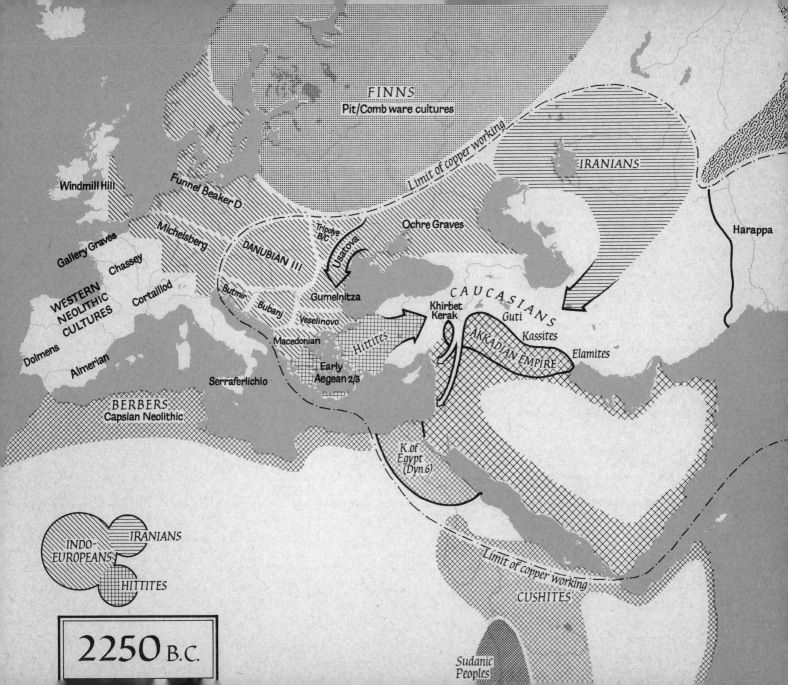

FINNS
Pit/Comb ware cultures

Limit of copper working

IRANIANS

Windmill Hill

Funnel Beaker D

Gallery Graves

Michelsberg

Ochre Graves

Chassey

DANUBIAN III

Tripolye B/C

Usatova

Harappa

WESTERN
NEOLITHIC
CULTURES

Cortaillod

Butmir

Bubanj

Gumelnitza

C A U C A S I A N S

Dolmens

Almerian

Veselinovo

Khirbet
Kerak

Guti

Kassites

Macedonian

AKKADIAN EMPIRE

Elamites

Serraferlichio

Early
Aegean 2/3

Hittites

BERBERS
Capsian Neolithic

K. of
Egypt
(Dyn. 6)

INDO-
EUROPEANS

IRANIANS

Limit of copper working

HITTITES

CUSHITES

2250 B.C.

Sudanic
Peoples

This map is of the same date as the last, but it is solely concerned with the three literate civilizations of the period, the Sumero-Akkadian, with its Elamite offshoot, the Egyptian and the Harappan. Each of these three valley systems probably contained about three quarters of a million people, the population density being higher than that in neolithic Europe by a factor of at least ten. The towns shown would have had populations in the 10–15,000 range. There were probably no more of this size than indicated; certainly there were none outside these three areas.

The discovery of an exotic artefact or material during an excavation often tempts the archaeologist into talk of trade routes; but given the small size and limited technology of these early communities, it is unreasonable to expect formal trade routes to be anything but exceptional as yet. A series of purely local and accidental exchanges can carry an article many hundreds of miles from its place of origin, and semi-precious substances – such as lapis lazuli, a favourite in the trade route game as its site of sole occurrence in Afghanistan is well known – would travel all the further for being at a discount in the area where they were found and at a premium away from it. In fact, the barbarians' appetite for the townsman's products must have greatly exceeded the townsman's craving for lapis lazuli and one can guess that the barbarians' main offerings were gold-dust and surplus progeny. Such exchanges as took place did not lead to the appearance of a merchant class, for they were fixed-price affairs, regulated by temple or palace. Similarly, when there was a shortage of necessary material, the response of Sargonid Mesopotamia, as of Egypt, was not merchant venturing but the mounting of a military expedition. Such were the Sargonid 'campaigns' among the timber-yielding mountains of the Lebanon, and the Egyptian excursions to the copper mines of Sinai. Beyond this range bilateral arrangements were necessary, as between Egypt and the Lebanon, but even this trading was Soviet-style, Pharaoh's representative negotiating with Lebanese sheik.

There is no evidence for sustained contact between Egypt and Mesopotamia but surprisingly there does seem to have been a tenuous link between Mesopotamia and the Indus valley by sea via Bahrein. The Mesopotamians exchanged their oil and textiles for Bahreini dates and for copper (from Oman or Ormuz?); exactly what commodities made the Bahreinis' journey to India worth while remains obscure; a possible answer is ivory.

The beginnings of literacy, the third topic of this section, are to be found in the tally, more particularly in the compound tally in which there is a simple drawing to show each class of object with which the tally is concerned; however, true literacy is reached only with the communication of ideas. One obvious way of doing this is to represent the idea by one of its pictorial aspects: we can draw a leg as a pictogram for *leg*, or as an ideogram for *go*. Another, better, way is to take the sound of the word represented by a pictogram and apply it to a similar sounding word of quite different meaning. In the sentence 'I am X with you', 'X' is a phonogram. Context would usually make it possible to distinguish between the different senses of O as a pictogram (sun), ideogram (day), and phonogram (son). Sumerians, who used all three classes, made certain of the sense by adding unpronounced signs called determinatives. Once again, they used both of the immediately obvious methods: the class determinative (O + man = son) and the phonetic determinative (O + pray = day). A script involving these methods is called *transitional*. The Sumerian prototype was in existence at the end of the fourth millennium and imitations (using new symbols and consequently looking as different from Sumerian as they do from each other) were in use in Elam and Egypt soon after 3000.

Clay tablets were the characteristic writing material of Mesopotamia and it is better to impress clay than to incise it. The Sumerians soon took to impressing their signs with a stylus which, being triangular in section, left a wedge-shaped (cuneiform) mark. With the change to the cuneiform method, Sumerian writing lost its pictorial quality. The Akkadians took over the developed Sumerian system for their own language and in the second half of the third millennium the Elamites followed suit, abandoning their own transitional script. For everyday use the Egyptians, who wrote with brush and ink on papyrus, similarly simplified their own hieroglyphic[1] writing into the cursive form known as 'hieratic', but the hieroglyphs were retained for formal inscriptions.

The Indus valley script is presumed to be transitional and an imitation of the Sumerian, though it has not been deciphered.

---

1. Hieroglyphic simply means 'priestly writing' and indicates the religious monopoly of literacy in ancient Egypt. By (etymologically incorrect) analogy, any form of writing which has a high pictorial content is apt to be called hieroglyphic, but in this sense the term hieroglyphic says nothing about the system of writing involved. As far as system goes, the remarkable feature of the Egyptian script was that only the consonants were represented. Ths s jst pssbl n Nglsh, but works quite easily in Hamitic (and Semitic) languages.

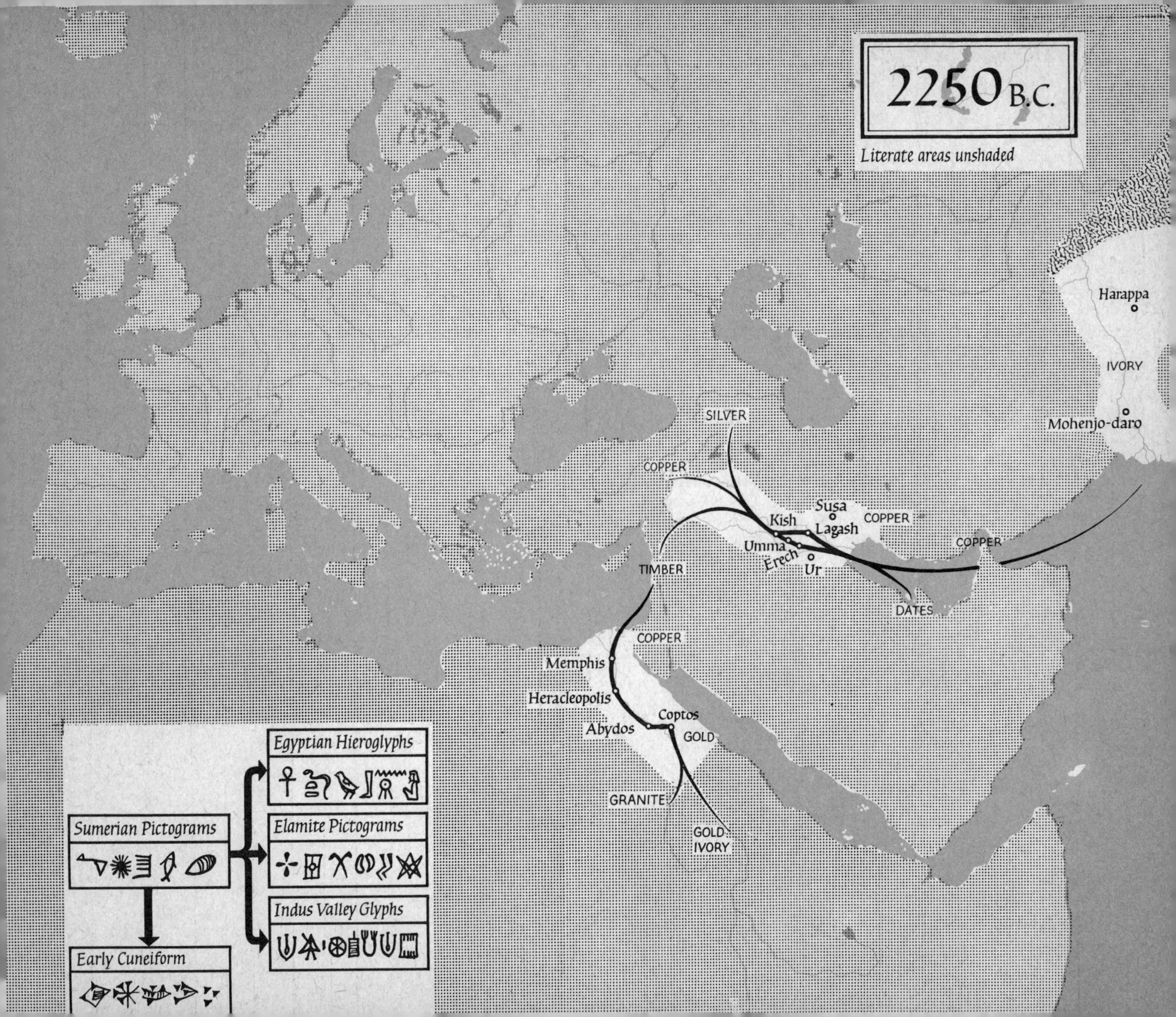

2250 B.C.
Literate areas unshaded
Harappa
IVORY
Mohenjo-daro
SILVER
COPPER
Susa
Kish
COPPER
Lagash
Umma
Erech
Ur
COPPER
TIMBER
DATES
COPPER
Memphis
Heracleopolis
Coptos
Abydos
GOLD
GRANITE
GOLD
IVORY
Egyptian Hieroglyphs
Sumerian Pictograms
Elamite Pictograms
Indus Valley Glyphs
Early Cuneiform

# 1850 B.C.

The Guti were finally expelled from Mesopotamia by the Sumerians of Erech (c.2100), but it was left to the Kings of Ur's famous third dynasty to re-establish the Sargonid frontiers and write the final chapter of Sumerian history. The dynasty lasted through the twenty-first century at the close of which the armies of Ur were overthrown by the Elamites and Amorites. For the next two centuries, Mesopotamia reverted to its archaic pattern of independent city states interpenetrated by nomadic tribes. All the names that survive from this period are Semitic; the Sumerians have been absorbed.

The Amorite expansion is the first overflow of Arabian nomads of which we have definite knowledge. It involved the whole of the fertile crescent and Amorite dynasties were established in all the important towns – Damascus, Aleppo, Mari, Assur, Babylon and Isin. The Elamites expelled the Amorites from the southernmost town of Sumer, Larsa, and it is the resultant Amorite–Elamite rivalry that has given its name to this (Isin-Larsa) period of Mesopotamian history. It would be less parochial to call it Amorite.

By subduing the Heracleopolitans, c. 2050, the Theban princes of the eleventh dynasty re-united Egypt and initiated the 'Middle Kingdom': (middle in time; it comes between the Old Kingdom and the New or Empire). With the accession of the twelfth dynasty a few years later and the transfer of the capital to Memphis, the Middle Kingdom began to surpass the Old in splendour. The southern frontier was advanced to the second cataract, while Cis-Jordanian Palestine and the sea ports of the Lebanon seem to have accepted a considerable degree of Pharaonic direction. Trans-Jordan, which had previously been cultivated, now passed into the possession of nomads; presumably this was another facet of the Amorite migration.

At this period we have documentary proof of Hittite dominance in Anatolia; their kindred in western Anatolia were the Luvians. The *Minoans* of Crete and the Pelasgians of Greece are now usually thought of as belonging to the Hittite group, but in the present state of Aegean studies this can be no more than a reasonable assumption.[1]

The spread of a characteristic artefact can be explained either by the diffusion of an idea or by the migration of a people who were its sole manufacturers. The difference between the two modes is not altogether sharp even in theory, for ideas are spread by example, and in archaeological practice the distinction is often dishearteningly difficult to make. The spread of the megalithic tomb would seem to be a fair example of diffusion with a minimum of migration, for communal vaults of this type (using large, undressed stones) appear across Western Europe at the close of the third millennium without otherwise modifying the local cultures. Because their laborious construction implies a new and compelling system of beliefs, and because they continued in use through many later upheavals, archaeologists tend to talk in terms of a 'megalithic religion'. On the other hand, the similarly wide distribution attained by *bell-beaker* pottery at a period not long after this has long been taken to indicate the spread of a distinct people. The standardized equipment of the *bell-beaker* graves forces one to accept this, but when one considers the direction of the movement, one enters an area of controversy. The *bell-beaker folk* march convincingly in every prehistorian's text, but they do so from Spain to Germany in some and from Germany to Spain in others, while lately there has been a tendency to make them go from Spain to Germany and back again (primary and reflux movements). The only firm datum seems to be that the British *beaker folk* came from the Rhine–Elbe region and not from Brittany, which favours the westward interpretation. The main reason for taking an exclusively westward view, however, is that the *bell-beaker* distribution map resembles the Celto-Ligurian world of a millennium later too exactly for coincidence, and, if the equation of *beaker-folk* with Celto-Ligurians is accepted, the expansion must have been westward, from the Indo-European zone.

The existence of the Celto-Ligurians as an entity at this time has other, important consequences. The Indo-Europeans are divided by philologists into two groups, Eastern and Western, with Teutons, Celto-Ligurians, Italics and Illyrians forming the Western group. If we can identify the Celto-Ligurians, the East/West division must also have been in existence. We can postulate a line for this which is consistent with later evidence and carries the conviction of simplicity; each of the remaining members of the Western phylum then receives the geographical isolation necessary for its further speciation: Teutonic in Scandinavia, Italic in Italy and Illyrian in Yugoslavia.[2]

The peoples between Scandinavia and the Urals were at this time in a cultural phase characterized by the presence of ritual *battle-axes* in their burials. Though the distribution of this rite – basically

(continued on page 92)

1. Minoan is an invented term, derived from the heroic age of King Minos of Crete, who would in fact have been a Mycenaean Greek, not a pre-Greek; Pelasgian is a word used by the Greeks for the people they found in possession when they first moved into the peninsula (probably about this time, possibly not until 1600), though they sometimes spoilt the sense by using it for pre-Dorian Greeks.
2. With the Ligurians, who in the sixth century are in occupation of the Atlantic coasts of Spain and France and the Italian and French rivieras, we can bracket the Corsicans and Sardinians and the Q-Celts of Ireland. The orthodox view that the distribution of Q-Celts as well as P-Celts (the distinction is philological) is explained by the *Urnfield* expansion of the first half of the last millennium B.C., I find inadequate; for Ireland, Q-Celtic in Roman times, never received more than a minor *Urnfield* component; Scotland at the same period was occupied by the descendants of the earliest *Urnfield* wave, yet they spoke P-Celtic like the final arrivals. It seems simplest to see the *Urnfield* expansion as entirely P-Celtic and the archaic Q-Celtic of Ireland as a survival of the preceding migratory movement, that of the *beaker-folk*.

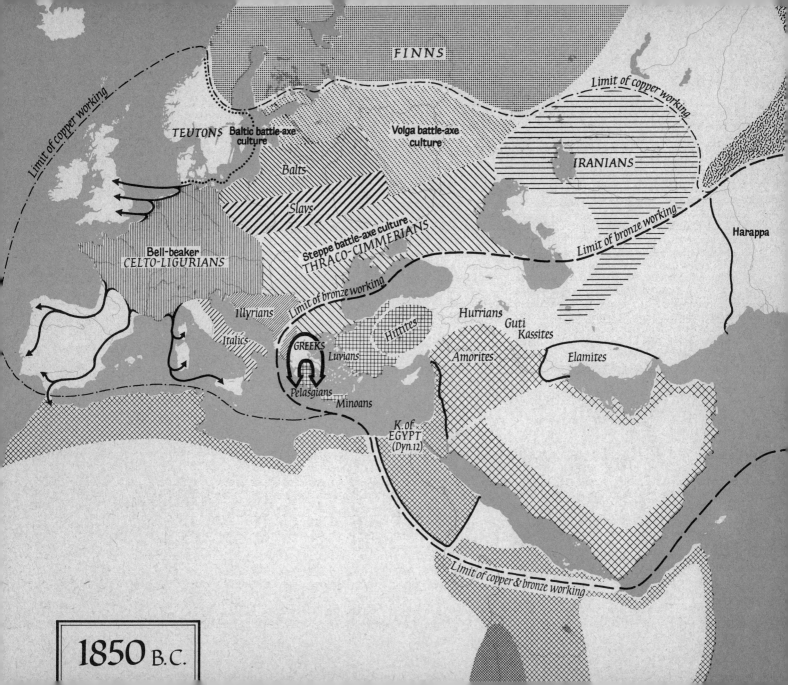

FINNS

Limit of copper working

TEUTONS   Baltic battle-axe
culture

Volga battle-axe
culture

Limit of copper working

Balts

IRANIANS

Slavs

Steppe battle-axe culture
THRACO-CIMMERIANS

Limit of bronze working

Bell-beaker
CELTO-LIGURIANS

Harappa

Illyrians

Limit of bronze working

Hurrians

Italics

Guti
Kassites

GREEKS

Hittites

Luvians

Amorites

Elamites

Pelasgians

Minoans

K. of
EGYPT
(Dyn.12)

Limit of copper & bronze working

1850 B.C.

In the eighteenth century the third in the long succession of Mesopotamian empires was created by the Amorite Hammurabi of Babylon, author of the famous 'eye for an eye' law code. His successors had to contend with increasing pressure from the Caucasian Hurrians in the north, from the Kassites of the Zagros in the east and from the King of the 'Sea Land' in the south, but they hung on in Akkad for a century and it was a newcomer who finally extinguished the dynasty. Starting about 1600, Mursilis, third king of the united Hittites, took his army on annual forays south of the Taurus. Aleppo, the strongest of the Syrian principalities, was taken; then he reached down the Euphrates to Babylon. Its sack was the culminating point in the history of the first Hittite Empire, which collapsed on Mursilis' death. Into the power vacuum which he left flowed enemies more familiar to the Mesopotamians; the south of the country was occupied by the King of the Sea Land, the central third by the Kassites, the north, together with Syria, by the Hurrians.

In Egypt also, political unity was a thing of the past. Under the thirteenth dynasty, the rift between Upper and Lower Egypt opened again; then each half split into warring principalities, with Thebes in the lead in the south and Xois in the delta. At this moment of weakness (c.1700), the country suffered its first historical invasion, that of the Semitic nomads known as the Hyksos. Much ink has been spilt on the nature of the Hyksos movement; it is probably fair to regard it as the final upheaval in the Amorite series. The Hyksos kingdom (dynasties fifteen and sixteen) consisted of Palestine and the delta and probably exacted homage from the native princes who survived upriver at Thebes (dynasty seventeen). The migration of the clan of Abraham from the bend of the fertile crescent is usually, and plausibly, referred to the first period of Amorite expansion; Joseph's successful move into Egypt to the time of the Hyksos pharaohs, with their presumably favourable attitude to Semitic immigrants. The term 'Hebrew' (Apiru) is used by Egyptians of the second millennium to describe all aliens of nomadic habits and only became a specific designation after the Exodus.

If, for Egypt and Mesopotamia, this was a time of foreign domination, the outward forms of their already ancient civilizations were respected and soon adopted by their conquerors. The inhabitants of the Indus Valley were not so fortunate, for the *Harappan* culture was utterly destroyed in the Aryan (Iranian) invasion. As a civilization it had not been very remarkable, its techniques being imported and never improved, its buildings utilitarian and its artefacts unattractive, and the completeness of its destruction is its only real claim to fame. Whereas many of the monuments and much of the lore of Egypt and Mesopotamia survived their overthrow, the culture of the Indus valley is known to us through archaeology alone.

In the *Rig-veda*, the Aryans have left a fairly full picture of an early Indo-European horde of the stock-breeding type. The most significant addition to the repertoire at this time is the horse-drawn chariot, and that this invention was already widely disseminated through the Indo-European area is shown by its representation on Greek grave stones of the sixteenth century.[1] The chariot as a fighting vehicle put the Indo-Europeans at a great advantage *vis-à-vis* the foot soldiers of the settled Near Eastern communities, an advantage that was quickly exploited. The Hurrians and Kassites were Caucasians, but it is known that clans of Iranian charioteers played a leading part in the society that resulted from the sixteenth-century upheaval. The Mitanni who moved into northern Mesopotamia at this time[2] and eventually became the suzerains of the Hurrians, are typical Iranians, and though we do not have a tribal designation for the sixteenth-century rulers of the Kassites, their names show that they also were of Iranian stock.

However, attempts to show that the Hyksos (who introduced the chariot into Egypt) contained a significant Indo-European component, are now regarded with disfavour.

Quite as important as their movements into Iran and India was the Iranians' expansion via the Ili and Tarim basins across central Asia, an expansion that must have been well under way at this period and was to proceed steadily until, by 500 B.C., Iranian tribes stretched in unbroken sequence from the Danube to the borders of China.

In Europe the major event is the spread of bronze-working across the continent. The comparatively settled period that followed the *bell-beaker* expansion favoured the differentiation of many local variants of the European early bronze style.[3] Scandinavia, South-Western France and Atlantic Spain remained at a chalcolithic level,[4] while North Africa stagnated in the neolithic until the arrival of the Phoenicians. In Spain we can allot the Iberians at least as large an area as they held when the historical record opens (which is after the passage of a further wave of Celts).

1. The Greeks were in possession of their peninsula by 1600 at the latest. For diagrammatic reasons, they are not given the Indo-European shading they should logically have.

2. As a salutary instance of the degree of supposition involved in arguments about prehistory, it is worth noting that the appearance of the Iranian and Aryan invaders in Mesopotamia and India is the first *proof* of the presence of Indo-Europeans on the plateau between.

3. Contemporary sub-divisions of the European bronze age are: British Isles: *Food vessel* (North) and *Wessex* (South); France: *Amorican* (North-West) and *Rhône* (South); Central Europe: *Unetice*; Mediterranean Spain: *El Argar*; Sicily: *Castellucio*; Malta: *Tarxien*; Italy: *Apennine A*; Yugoslavia: *Vatin*; Aegean: *Late Helladic (Minoan) I*.

4. The use of a line to show the limit of chalcolithic technology is discontinued at this point. Neither chalcolithic nor bronze-making techniques crossed the Sahara or travelled further up the Nile than the Sudd marshes; Negro Africa remained at a neolithic level until its Iron Age began (see page 50, Note 2).

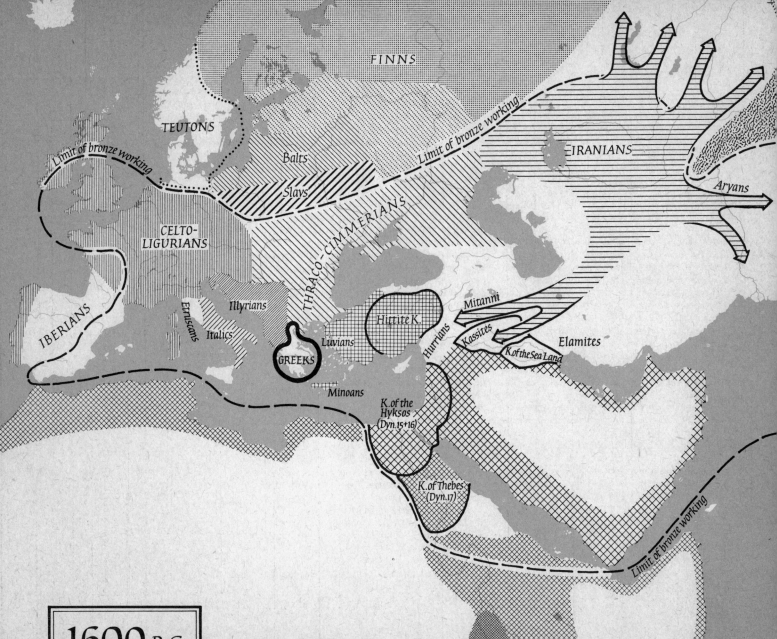

FINNS

TEUTONS

Balts

Slays

*Limit of bronze working*

*Limit of bronze working*

IRANIANS

Aryans

CELTO-
LIGURIANS

THRACO-CIMMERIANS

IBERIANS

Etruscans

Illyrians

Italics

GREEKS

Luvians

Hittite K.

Mitanni

Hurrians

Kassites

K. of the Sea Land

Elamites

Minoans

K. of the
Hyksos
(Dyn.15+16)

K. of Thebes
(Dyn.17)

*Limit of bronze working*

## 1600 B.C.

# 1300 B.C.

The expulsion of the Hyksos from Egypt by the prince of Thebes transformed the vassal seventeenth dynasty into the Imperial eighteenth. The liberation of the country was immediately followed by a successful onslaught on the Palestinian remainder of the Hyksos dominion, while succeeding pharaohs went further, Tutmosis I raiding among the Hurrians of Syria (1500)[1], and Tutmosis III making the Euphrates his frontier and on occasions crossing it (1450). However, a counter-offensive by the Hurrians under the leadership of the Mitanni succeeded in driving the Egyptians from Syria, and thereafter the eighteenth dynasty Empire never extended much beyond Palestine. The truce between the Egyptians and Mitanni, at first sullen, became cordial as the power of the Hittites revived. In the second quarter of the fourteenth century the Hittites brought the states of Western Anatolia under control;[2] towards its end Hittite armies appeared south of the Taurus once more. The invaders quickly broke the power of the Mitanni and annexed northern Syria. The Assyrians took advantage of the Hittite victories to shake off Mitannian overlordship but found themselves, for safety's sake, supporting their late masters as the Hittites moved east across the Euphrates. They were held, and a diminished Mitannian state lived on as the buffer of Assyria.

Far from taking advantage of the collapse of the Mitannian rule in Syria, Egypt, preoccupied with the religious revolution of Akhenaton, allowed her Palestinian province to drift to the edge of obedience. It was only with the victory of the traditional priesthood and the accession of a new dynasty eager to revive the splendours of the Tutmosid Empire, that Egypt intervened in Syria. But the nineteenth dynasty's most militant pharaohs, Seti I and Rameses II, were both beaten off by the Hittites, the latter in a decisive battle at

Kadesh (1280). Rameses II is the usual choice for pharaoh of the Exodus because the Hebrews toiled on extensions to Avaris, the old Hyksos capital which Rameses renamed after himself. Many 'Apiru' are attested among his slave labourers; their revolt and escape is the real beginning of Jewish history. The Hebrews took a route across the south of Edom, then east of Moab, the entry to the promised land being made via the southernmost and weakest of the Amorite principalities, Gilead.

In the bend of the fertile crescent we now find the Amorites replaced by the Aramaeans; in Mesopotamia the Kingdom of the Sea Land has been extinguished by the Kassites. The Minoan Kingdom of Knossos and the eteoCypriote Kingdom of Alasia[3] have both fallen to the Greeks; the petty kings of peninsular Greece acknowledge the overlordship of the King of Mycenae, those of Crete and the islands the new dynasts of Knossos. Greek rule beyond these areas is very problematical, but a reasonable case has been made for Miletus.

In darker Europe the notable event is the appearance of the *Lausitz* culture in Poland. The *Lausitz* folk were the first to adopt a funeral rite soon to become widespread: cremation with burial of the ashes in an urn. Archaeologists term the cemetery that results from this practice an urnfield, and the community concerned an urnfield culture. A pioneering attitude towards the disposal of its loved ones is not the only distinction of the *Lausitz* culture for its evolution was for long equated with the genesis of the Slav peoples. However, it is now accepted that the Bronze Age cultures of the middle Dnieper were equally Slav. The *Lausitz* culture therefore represents the differentiation of the western branch of the Slavs, separated from their eastern kin by the Pripet marshes.

About 1500 northern China passed straight from the neolithic into a full Bronze Age. The absence of an evolutionary chalcolithic phase confirms the obvious assumption that the Chinese derived their bronze-working techniques from the Near East.

Contemporary sub-divisions of the European Bronze Age are: British Isles: *Cinerary Urns* (North) and *Wessex* (South); France: *Armorican* (North-West) and *Rhône* (South); Mediterranean France and Northern Italy: *Terramare 1*; Central Europe: *Tumuli B*; Mediterranean Spain: *El Argar*; Sicily and Malta: *Thapsos*; Italy: *Apennine B*; Yugoslavia: *Vatin*; Aegean: *Late Helladic (Minoan) III B*.

1. Tutmosis I also conquered Nubia as far as the fourth cataract.
2. The most important of these was the Kingdom of Arzawa which corresponds to the later Lydia. Mention is also made of Lukka, which sounds like Lycia and of something that could well be Troy. In passing it is worth noting that the second Hittite dynasty was Hattite by blood.
3. The Greeks of the period are called Achaeans by historians with a literary bias, Mycenaeans by those with archaeological leanings. The eteoCypriotes are the pre-Greek population of Cyprus; their writing is sufficiently similar to Minoan to be sometimes termed Cypro-Minoan but this of course does not necessitate any linguistic relationship and their ethnic affinities remain undetermined.

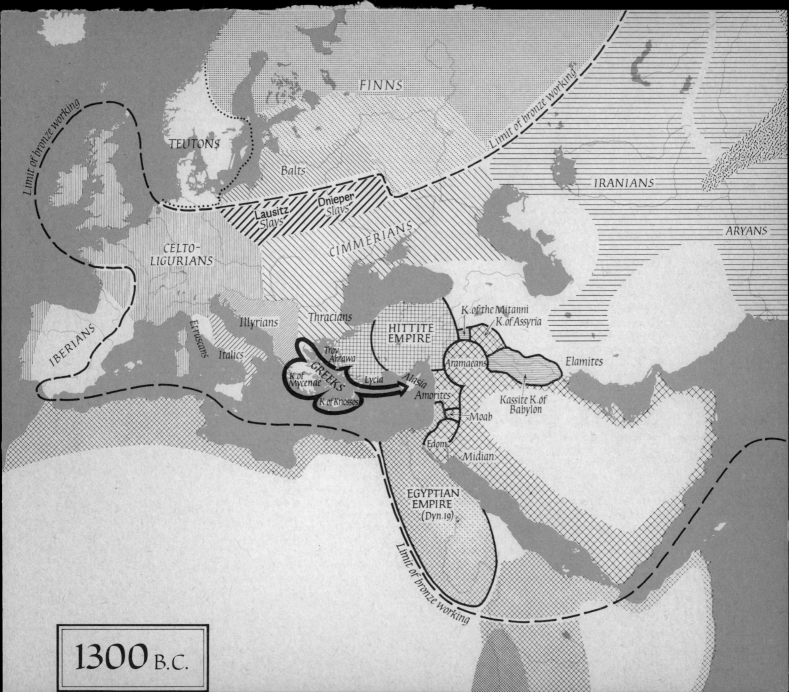

FINNS

TEUTONS

Balts

*Limit of bronze working*

*Limit of bronze working*

IRANIANS

ARYANS

Lausitz
Slavs

Dnieper
Slavs

CELTO-
LIGURIANS

CIMMERIANS

Etruscans

Illyrians

Thracians

IBERIANS

Italics

Troy
Arzawa

GREEKS

K.of
Mycenae

Lycia

K.of Knossos

Alasia

HITTITE
EMPIRE

K.of the Mitanni
K.of Assyria

Aramaeans

Elamites

Kassite K.of
Babylon

Amorites

Moab

Edom

Midian

EGYPTIAN
EMPIRE
(Dyn.19)

*Limit of bronze working*

# 1300 B.C.

In the thousand years that separate this map from the previous one on these topics, the only significant addition to the civilized area is off the map, in northern China. There, by 1300, the Shang kings were ruling a vigorous urban society and their priests were beginning to use a transitional script that is as clearly dependent on Near Eastern prototypes as it is ancestral to modern Chinese. Within our area, Anatolia and the Aegean have been added to the literate zone, but they only counter-balance the loss of the Indus valley and their literacy was to prove but temporary. The promise of the Bronze Age had, in fact, been largely fulfilled within a few centuries of its opening and, while China made its great leap forward, the West remained for a cycle in Cathay.

If there was little change in the population or prosperity of the Near East as a whole, within it there was a decline in southern Mesopotamia and a rise in Syria and Palestine. Increasing use of irrigation, causing a rise in the water-table, has been convincingly advanced as the reason for south Mesopotamian decline, for the water-table is saline and agricultural yields fall as salinity rises. The second millennium was a period of relative eclipse for Mesopotamia south of Babylon. Slower but steadier population growth resulted from the non-irrigating agriculture of Palestine and Syria, and in these areas the Bronze Age optimum was only attained in the second half of the period; the Fertile Crescent thus came into rough balance. As before, the towns shown are those it is reasonable to suppose achieved populations in the 10–15,000 range.

At the close of the third millennium, tin reappears in Mesopotamia. If, as is probable, the new source of supply was in Transcaucasia, the opening of traffic with the north coincides neatly with the first stirrings of Assyria, the routes' natural entrepôt. At a later date (nineteenth century), we know that the Assyrians controlled Mesopotamia's trade with Anatolia, for we have the records of the permanent delegation they maintained in the Anatolian town of Kanesh. This official body with extra-territorial rights arranged the export of Anatolian copper and the import from Assyria of tin and textiles; carriage was by donkey-train and values were reckoned in silver according to standard Mesopotamian practice. The policing of the nearer parts of these routes foreshadows and explains the Assyrians' recurrent attempts at military expansion in the later second millennium; the increasing impetus behind this expansion is a measure of the rising importance of trade.

Outside this clear example, the second millennium again has little to add to the third; there is a little iron (also from Anatolia), but it is so costly – forty times silver by weight – as to be the prerogative of kings; Egypt's isolation is still only broken intermittently, with trips to the Lebanon for timber, or to Eritrea and Arabia. Much has been written on the Achaeans as traders, and in the Levant, where they held Cyprus, such traffic as went on was probably carried in Greek hulls as often as Syrian. Cyprus had displaced Anatolia as the main source of copper[1] and a fairly steady trade in wine, oil and textiles in addition is possible if not proven. But for Achaean activity in the seas around Greece proper, the analogy suggested by legend is to the Vikings rather than the Hanse; it was a hornet's nest that Paris robbed, not a hive of honey-grubbers. Archaeology and palaeography agree: the cities sung by Homer are revealed by the spade as no more than citadels while the Achaeans' surviving accounts proclaim their simple self-sufficiency. Their ships certainly reached as far west as Sicily, which is enough to make them responsible for such exchanges as took place between Europe and the Orient at the time, Egyptian faience and Baltic amber being known examples of this; but something more than the barter of baubles by pirates is required if the Mycenaean thalassocracy is to be given the predominantly commercial colouring so often bestowed on it and, for that matter, on its entirely parochial predecessor, the Minoan. West of Greece, the evidence so far suggests a state of affairs only one degree better than drift.

1. Recently, skin-diving archaeologists have discovered and excavated a ship that went down around 1200 off Cape Gelidonya (on the southern coast of Turkey). The vessel was small, only twenty-seven feet in length; it was carrying a ton of copper ingots and scrap from Cyprus and also some tin, perhaps half a hundredweight. The tin must have been taken aboard at some Levantine port, but presumably derived ultimately from Transcaucasia.

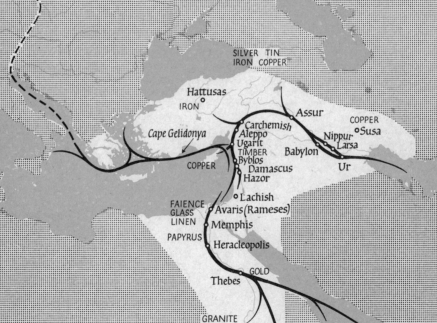

AMBER

SILVER TIN
IRON COPPER

Hattusas
IRON

Cape Gelidonya

Carchemish
Aleppo
Ugarit
TIMBER
Byblos
Damascus
Hazor

COPPER

Assur

COPPER
Susa
Nippur
Larsa
Babylon

Ur

Lachish

FAIENCE
GLASS
LINEN

Avaris (Rameses)

Memphis

PAPYRUS

Heracleopolis

GOLD

Thebes

GRANITE

IVORY
RESINS

RESINS

GOLD
IVORY

While the Indus valley script was being swept into oblivion by the Aryan invasion, cuneiform, first carried into Anatolia by the Assyrian traders, was adapted to the Hittite, Luvian and Hattite languages. The Amorites, Hurrians and Mitanni of Syria followed suit in succeeding centuries and even the pharaohs of the proud eighteenth dynasty conducted their foreign correspondence in cuneiform (and in the Akkadian language, the recognized diplomatic mode of the era). But if outwardly the second millennium was the heyday of cuneiform, from about the beginning of the sixteenth century the original transitional scripts had been rendered technically obsolete by the appearance of the open syllabary. Being a collection of puns, cuneiform and Egyptian hieroglyphic contain signs for all types of monosyllable and even some signs for disyllables. The open syllabaries have signs for syllables of the consonant–vowel type only, a rationalization that reduces the number needed from hundreds to a mere eighty or so. The Hittites, eteoCypriotes and Minoans each created open syllabaries of their own. Because they wanted their monumental inscriptions to look impressive in the Egyptian manner, the Hittites made their script heavily pictorial; consequently it is called Hittite hieroglyphic. The eteoCypriote[1] is little known, but appears to be ancestral to the Minoan which passes through an early hieroglyphic stage to a more rapidly written 'Linear A'. When the Achaeans conquered the Aegean area, they modified Linear A in order to use it for the writing of Greek, the result being the recently deciphered Linear B. The ancestor of all these open syllabaries has been sought in the 'pseudo-hieroglyphs' of Byblos, but the dating and decipherment of these is too unsteady as yet to permit much theorizing.

The open syllabary was in its turn outmoded by the consonantal alphabet, a Syro-Palestinian invention that followed naturally from the use of an open syllabary for writing a language like Semitic in which the vowels occur in regular relation to the consonants. When this is the case, only one sign is required for each class in the syllabary – one for m (any vowel) for example – and the total number of signs needed falls to about twenty. This is such an epoch-making advance that it seems petty to point out that a set of signs for consonants (any vowel) is not the same as a set consisting of separate signs for consonants and vowels and that a consonantal alphabet is not a true alphabet.

There are consonantal alphabets both in cuneiform (Ugaritic script) and in a cursive based on Egyptian hieroglyphs (early Canaanite and Sinai scripts). The surprising thing about them is their date, some examples of early Canaanite being put as far back as the eighteenth century. This makes it entirely possible that the evolutionary sequence from open syllabary to consonantal alphabet given here is false, and that the open syllabary was in fact an expanded version of the consonantal alphabet for languages in which vowels were unpredictable.

1. The presumption that eteoCypriote and Minoan are open syllabaries is based on the number of signs they employ, for neither can be read. Nor can another Cretan syllabary, that of the Phaistos disk, an isolated find but a fascinating one in that its signs are impressed with punches. This was the nearest anyone was to get to printing for the next two thousand years.

Hittite Hieroglyphs

Hittite, Mitannian, Elamite, Amorite, Assyrian-Akkadian Cuneiform scripts

Cypro-Minoan script

Cretan Linear scripts

Byblos script

Egyptian Hieroglyphs

Egyptian Hieratic

Sinai script

Ugaritic script

# 1200 B.C.

About 1200 the Achaean Greek and Hittite kingdoms were overthrown by migrating barbarians. This movement started in the south-east of the Balkans with two peoples, the Dorian Greeks and the Phrygians. The Dorians, the northernmost of the Greek tribes, broke into the peninsula and methodically sacked the Achaean strongholds; they then took to the sea and meted out the same treatment in Crete and Rhodes. The Phrygians, a Thracian people who crossed to Anatolia in the middle of the thirteenth century, were held in the north-eastern corner by the Hittites until 1200 when, in company with the Luvians, they broke out and overthrew the Hittite state. Though the Phrygians certainly crossed the Taurus, it is the Luvians who seem to have played the major part in the second stage of the upheaval – the invasion and colonization of Syria – for when the dust settles there are plenty of Luvian (neo-Hittite) principalities in Syria, but no Phrygian ones.

The protagonists in the third stage are more difficult to identify. In the 1180s, a horde of what the Egyptians called 'sea-peoples' overran Palestine and was only beaten back with difficulty from Egypt itself (by Rameses III, first pharaoh of the twentieth dynasty). Thwarted but still far from impotent, the 'sea-peoples' settled in coastal Palestine and lorded it over their neighbours – Israelites, Canaanites and Phoenicians – to whom they were known as Philistines.[1] We are uncertain as to the identity of the sea-peoples: the likely candidates are not the initiators of the twelfth-century *Volkwanderung*, the Phrygians and Dorians (the latter in any case are excluded by the equation of Philistine with Pelasgian), but the secondary migrators among whom we must include the Achaeans as well as the Luvians. Egyptian records give Cilician origins for some of the sea peoples which favours the Luvian side, but is not entirely decisive in that the Achaeans dominated the southern coast of Anatolia at this time. The Achaean case is strengthened by the Egyptian stress on the naval power of the horde, by the Philistines' own legend of their Cretan origin and by close parallels between Philistine and Mycenaean pottery.

The dark age that the barbarian invaders brought to the Aegean and Anatolia was to last for some four centuries; in the fertile crescent, they deprived Egypt for ever of her Palestinian province and humbled the Assyrians. At the close of the thirteenth century Assyria had been lording it over Syria and Babylon; now the Kassite dynasty revived.[2]

In Europe a new series of *Urnfield* cultures was evolving along the Rhine and upper Danube. This group is agreed by all to be Celtic; in my view, it is specifically P-Celtic. The necessary corollary to the definition of the Celts is the restriction of the term Ligurian to the peoples west and south of the Rhine, in France and north-west Spain. The Ligurian culture of north-east Italy (*Terramare 2*) was absorbed into the Italic (*Apennine D*) during this period.

The spread of bronze working to Scandinavia and northern Russia brings the whole area shown (except for a still neolithic North Africa) into the Bronze Age; accordingly, the line showing the limits of the technique can be dropped.

The Trojan War must have been the last fling of the Achaeans. Priam speaks of having fought in his youth on the side of the Phrygians against 'Amazons', who could well be the beardless Hittites. This would fit the situation existing in the second half of the thirteenth century.

1. Canaanite refers to the population (and language) of inland Syria–Palestine, Phoenician to that of the Lebanese littoral: they are sub-divisions of Amorite.
2. The Kassites were finally swept away by the Elamites in the mid twelfth century.

38

FINNS

TEUTONS

Balts

Lausitz Slavs · Dneiper Slavs

Urnfield CELTS

CIMMERIANS

IBERIANS

Etruscans · Illyrians · Thracians

Phrygians

Dorian Greeks

Italics · Luvians

Sicans

Achaean Greeks

K. of the Mitanni
K. of Assyria

Aramaeans

K. of Elam

Israel
Moab

Philistines

Edom

Midian

K. of
EGYPT
(Dyn. 20)

**1200** B.C.

# 1000 B.C.

No sooner had the Near East taken on a semblance of stability again, with the settling down of the neo-Hittites (Luvians) and Philistines, than the Aramaeans spilt over the fertile crescent. A second Assyrian empire (the creation of Tiglath-Pileser I, who, at the beginning of the eleventh century, conquered Syria and Babylon) was swept away, Aramaean tribes moved into the pasture lands and one after another the towns began to fall to their sheiks. As with the Amorites, new dynasties arose in old principalities from Babylon to Damascus, but there was never any attempt to sum these individual successes into a larger political entity. The half-dozen tribes that invaded southern Mesopotamia were known collectively as Chaldeans; to call Abraham's Ur 'Chaldean' as the Bible does is thus anachronistic as well as geographically incorrect.[1]

The colonization of the west coast of Anatolia by the Ionian Greeks seems to have aroused little response from the Lydians[2] or their theoretical suzerains, the Phrygians. The Ionians claimed to be pre-Dorian but, judging by their dialect in later times, seem to fall somewhere between the true descendants of the Achaeans (in Cyprus, southern Anatolia and the inaccessible centre of the Peloponnese) and the Dorians (to the south of the Ionians, along the arc Peloponnese–Crete–Rhodes). These various dialects were to disappear in the freer intercourse of Hellenistic times when a development of Ionic became universal.

The pharaohs of the twentieth dynasty, all of whom took the prestigious name of Rameses, were weak creatures who never made any attempt to recover Palestine, and allowed first Thebes and then Tanis (the old Avaris/Rameses in the Delta) to become independent principalities. After the death of the last Ramesid (1085) the unity of the country was restored by a matrimonial pact between Tanite and Theban houses, but the pharaohs of this (twenty-first) dynasty remained feeble at home and helpless abroad. Nubia – the Nile valley between the first and fourth cataracts – became effectively independent.

During the political upheaval of the last quarter of the last millennium B.C., knowledge of iron-working techniques was disseminated throughout the Aegean–Near East area. About 1000 the Philistines were attempting to guarantee the military inferiority of the Hebrews by forbidding them to use the new metal, and the beginning of the last millennium B.C. is conventionally taken as the start of the Iron Age. The displacement of bronze by iron was, of course, a gradual process, begun before 1000 and not completed before the eighth century, but the convention is reasonable and a line showing the limits of the Iron Age world is introduced in this map.

The simple distribution of the Italics – all Italy west of a line drawn from the Central Alps to the Tiber – was modified by the arrival of the Illyrians on the Adriatic Coast and the departure of the Sicels from the toe. The nature of Sicily's aborigines, whom the Greeks called Sicans, is unknown. As *bell-beakers* have been found round Palermo, they could be Ligurian; an earlier wave of Italics is another obvious possibility and classical authors had it that one aboriginal group was Iberian.

In Europe there is nothing to note except the beginning of the westward expansion of the *Urnfield* Celts.

About this time the Iranians of the Transoxian region of Asia found that a skilful rider could manage his horse on the battlefield, a discovery that was ultimately to put an end to the chariot as a useful weapon.

1. See page 30, column 1.
2. Western Luvians, as were the Carians and Lycians to their south.

FINNS

TEUTONS

IRANIANS

Balts

Slavs

Urnfield CELTS

CIMMERIANS

Limit of iron working

Neo Hittites

Thracians

Lydians
Carians

K. of the Mitanni

Phrygians

K. of Assyria

Etruscans

Illyrians

IBERIANS

Ionians

Aramaeans

Elamites

Italics

GREEKS

Chaldaeans

Sicans

Sicels

Lycians

Phoenicians
Philistines

Ammon
Moab

Edom

Limit of iron working

K. of
Egypt
(Dyn. 21)

Midian

Nubia

1000 B.C.

Shortly after 1000, the Philistines' power was broken by the attacks (presumably concerted) of Phoenicians and Hebrews. The hitherto minor Phoenician town of Tyre sprang into prominence as the strongest and most enterprising in the Levant and the resurgence of Phoenicia was powered by the Tyrian discovery of Spain with its abundant minerals (c.1000). No more is heard of the Philistines at sea after this and on land they succumbed to the attacks of the Hebrews under the leadership of David in 975. David also forced Edom, Ammon, Moab and the principality of Damascus to recognize Hebrew overlordship, but this empire survived only as long as his son and successor Solomon (960–925); then the tributaries revolted and the Hebrew state itself split into the two Kingdoms of Judah and Israel, the first consisting of little more than David's capital Jerusalem, the second comprising the bulk of the Hebrew territory, but without a proper capital prior to the building of Samaria (880). Divided they were doomed. The first Pharaoh of the twenty-second dynasty, a Libyan mercenary who had replaced an impotent master, celebrated his accession with a razzia through Palestine which included a sack of Jerusalem (928), but there was no lasting revival on the part of Egypt and it was the Damascenes who made the Kings of Judah and Israel their vassals. Damascus, indeed, proved strong enough to stave off the otherwise irresistible Assyrians, who had re-established their control over northern Mesopotamia and reduced Babylon to dependency in the early ninth century and were now steadily advancing their frontier westward. Syria and Cilicia were subdued by Shalmaneser III (860–825) and this time the Assyrian had come to stay. The vigour, efficiency and number of their campaigns indicate the Assyrians' main difficulty; the area they sought to control, the northern half of the fertile crescent, lacked

natural defences. Punitive expeditions were mounted yearly: eastward against the Zagros tribes, southward against the ever rebellious Babylonians, northward against the recently established (c.875) Caucasian kingdom of Van, westward against the Aramaeans, neo-Hittites and even Phrygians. Victories were constantly celebrated; constant victory was the condition on which the Assyrian Empire existed.

Far more important in the long run than the story of Assyrian expansion was the colonization of the western Mediterranean by the Phoenicians and Greeks. About 800, the Phoenicians voyaging to Spain founded permanent stations on either side of the Sicilian channel, the half-way point on their route, and as Assyria bore down on Phoenicia the trading fleet increasingly based itself on these intermediate ports. Their growth was rapid, particularly in the case of Carthage (traditional foundation date, 814).

In Europe the pressure of the *Urnfield* Celts was still slowly building up. Continental immigrants to England at this time (*Deverel-Rimbury folk*), though not true *Urnfielders*, show evidence of contact with them and this contact presumably caused their move. In the south-west, *Urnfielders* had arrived at the gates of Spain.

Iron-working has now spread to Italy (the stepping-stone between Greece and western Europe), though it has barely begun in Egypt.

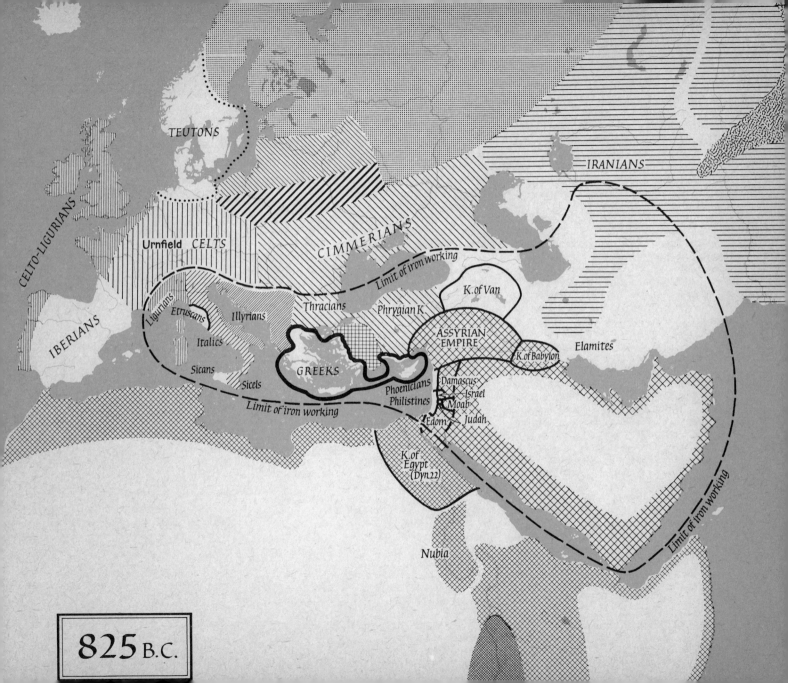

TEUTONS

IRANIANS

CELTO-LIGURIANS

Urnfield CELTS

CIMMERIANS

Limit of iron working

K. of Van

IBERIANS

Ligurians
Etruscans
Illyrians
Italics
Sicans
Sicels

Thracians

Phrygian K

ASSYRIAN
EMPIRE

K. of Babylon

Elamites

GREEKS

Phoenicians
Philistines

Damascus
Israel
Moab
Edom
Judah

Limit of iron working

K. of
Egypt
(Dyn.22)

Limit of iron working

Nubia

825 B.C.

In the ancient world the vast majority of towns served only local needs and their size was correspondingly limited;[1] towns marked as small circles on this and preceding maps are from the upper end of this range, having 10–15,000 inhabitants. By the ninth century, a few towns had grown to a size that requires a more emphatic symbol. As might be expected, four out of the five likely candidates for this distinction – which can be taken to imply a population of 30,000 or so – were capital cities, swollen by the presence of court and administration. Babylon and Memphis[2] had long been national centres; Nimrud and Nineveh, the twin Assyrian metropoli, were comparatively recent foundations that had come to overshadow the traditional capital Assur. As the Assyrian kings were the creators of the administered as opposed to merely tributary empire, so their cities were the first of really compelling magnitude; in its seventh-century heyday, the population of Nineveh may have reached the 100,000 mark.

The fifth of the major cities, Tyre, had grown to the first rank through commerce. Insignificant prior to the Achaean collapse of the twelfth century, she soon came to dominate the Phoenician revival that followed; as dependence on Phoenician merchants is still discernible when the mists of legend begin to clear away from the reviving Greek world of the eighth century, the Tyrians must have been in undisputed control of the Levantine routes for some three centuries. They made good use of their monopoly, trading their manufactures – glass, textiles and metal work – and their produce – timber, wine and oil – for Egyptian linen, papyrus, gold and ivory, Anatolian wool, Cypriot copper and Arabian resins. This traffic, steadily increasing in the early first millennium, established Tyre's prosperity, but it was the new range and volume that her discovery of Spain (c.1000) brought to Mediterranean

trade that made her great. The Iberian peninsula, henceforth the ancient world's major source of metal, provided the silver, copper and tin that guaranteed Phoenician, and in particular Tyrian, commercial hegemony in the Orient.

With the domestication of the camel in the twelfth century, the caravans characteristic of Arabian trade make their appearance. Those that made the transit between Palestine and Mesopotamia were simply carriers of Palestinian and Mesopotamian goods; the other major route – between Palestine and the Yemen via the Hejaz (= the corridor') – exported the resins that were Arabia's only significant product. Though these resins – myrrh, frankincense and balsam – were used in the ancient world as perfume, incense and medicine, and were highly esteemed in all roles, the Hejaz route can hardly have survived on resins alone. Many of the goods travelling north must have been re-exports deriving from East Africa and India.

In India, the first half of the last millennium brought a revival of urban life along the upper Ganges, but none that we know of on the Indus. However, the continuing darkness of the Indus valley is probably due only to lack of information for, in Assyrian times, contact was re-established between Mesopotamia and India and there must have been intermediaries of importance between the known Hindu centres on the Ganges and the seafarers who plied between Persian Gulf and Indus mouth. Later Indian exports consisted largely of spices, but at this stage we have little idea of what was traded, though, with the extinction of the Syrian elephant, ivory found in Mesopotamia can be confidently labelled an import and India seems as likely a source as Africa. One early result of this re-discovery of India was the introduction of the cotton plant to Mesopotamia.

Literacy has not made sufficient progress to require a separate map on this occasion. Transitional scripts continue in everyday use: hiero-

glyphic and hieratic in Egypt, cuneiform in Assyria, Babylonia, Van (newly literate), and Elam. Open syllabaries are still being written by the neo-Hittites (Hittite hieroglyphic) and Cypriots (for both Greek and eteoCypriote). The cuneiform alphabet has disappeared, the early Canaanite has evolved into the north Semitic and split into the Phoenician (with a distinct variant for Hebrew) and the Aramaic. South Arabia, the only important addition to the literate area, has its own alphabet derived from early Canaanite.

1. The average walled town of classical times covered 50–150 acres; a density of 100 inhabitants to the acre is a reasonable assumption though probably a slightly lower figure would be indicated for western Europe and a slightly higher one for the Near East.
2. The agricultural development of the Delta and the increasing involvement of Egypt in Mediterranean affairs resulted in a decline in the importance of Upper Egypt and the slow decay of Thebes.

**825 B.C.**

Literate area unshaded

COPPER SILVER TIN

IVORY SPICES

AMBER

WOOL

TIMBER

**Nineveh**
**Nimrud**
Assur

Susa

Carchemish
Aleppo
Hama

**Babylon**

COPPER

Erech
Ur

COPPER
Sidon
**Tyre**

TIMBER
Damascus

COPPER TIN SILVER

GLASS TEXTILES

Samaria

Gaza

Tanis

**Memphis**

PAPYRUS LINEN FAIENCE

GOLD

Thebes

IVORY RESINS

RESINS

GOLD IVORY

PHONETIC VALUES
ʼ b g d h w z ḥ ṭ i k l m n s ʻ p ṣ q r sh t

Phoenician script
𐤊 𐤂 𐤁 𐤀 ∃ Y I ⊟ ⊗ 𐤆 𐤈 𐤋 𐤌 𐤍 𐤎 ○ 𐤏 𐤒 𐤐 𐤓 w x

Aramaic script
𐡊 𐡂 𐡁 𐡀 ∃ Y I ⊟ ⊕ 𐡆 𐡈 𐡋 𐡌 𐡍 𐡎 ○ 𐡏 𐡒 𐡐 𐡓 w x

South Arabian script
𐩠 𐩬 𐩸 𐩹 Y ⌽ ⊗ 𐩳 Ⅲ 𐩲 𐩱 1 𐩮 𐩠 ○ ○ 𐩵 ) 3 X

In the first half of the eighth century, the Syrian and Cilician dependencies of Assyria were inspired to successful revolt by the kings of Van. However, the reign of Tiglath-Pileser III (745–728) saw Assyria make a more than complete recovery, and this time, instead of merely being required to pay and promise, defeated princes were replaced by governors-general. The term 'empire' thus gains the implication of direct rule which is usual hereafter. Tiglath-Pileser III advanced the Assyrian frontier beyond its previous limits, annexing Babylon in 729 and Damascus in 732. His successors continued this policy of the final solution in their dealings with rebels and enemies. When Israel refused tribute, its history was brought to an abrupt end by Sargon II (721–705), who sacked Samaria in the first year of his reign and deported the ten tribes that made up the northern Hebrew state. Judah, at first pro-Assyrian because Israel was anti, was seduced from her allegiance at the end of the century by Egyptian promises of liberation. Isaiah reasonably prophesied total disaster for both Judah and Egypt, but, as it turned out, Sennacherib (705–680) was forced to abandon his punitive campaign of 701 when the Angel of the Lord – without a word to Isaiah – struck down his army. This event, which a passage in Herodotus suggests may have been an outbreak of the plague, saved Jerusalem, but did not prevent Sennacherib from imposing an increase in tribute. Egypt's come-uppance was delivered by Esarhaddon (680–669) who invaded the country, annexed the delta and restricted the kings of the twenty-fifth (Nubian) dynasty[1] to the country up-river from Thebes (670).

On their northern frontier, the Assyrians received unexpected help from the Cimmerian and Scythian migrations. These movements began in the eighth century with a westward drive by the Iranians of Transoxiana, the tribes that moved into south Russia becoming known as Scyths, those that stayed behind as Sakas. The names are equivalent and there can be no doubt as to the homogeneity of this widespread nation which had evolved the culture of the horse-riding nomad that was to dominate the steppe from now on. A cause for the Scythian movement has been sought in the contemporary defeat of the Huns by the Chinese and their presumed recoil on the Iranians, but at this time the Huns were still foot-bound pastoralists, quite incapable of transmitting such pressure across the vastness of Asia. The same was true of the Cimmerians when first attacked by the Scyths. However, the rapid success of the refugee Cimmerian hordes that appeared south of the Caucasus at the end of the eighth century – they broke the power of the kingdom of Van, then turning west, overthrew the Phrygians – argues that they soon learnt to fight Scythian-style on horseback.[2]

The considerable body of Scyths that chased south after the Cimmerians came into conflict with their kinsmen, the Medes, whom they crushingly defeated. Like the Cimmerians' destructive passage through the Kingdom of Van, this was greatly to the Assyrians' advantage, for the Medes had now emerged as the leaders of the Iranians of the plateau and a major foe of the Assyrians. The Caucasian aborigines of the Zagros marches were now ground out of political existence by the bitter and continuous warfare between the two.

The first Greek colonies outside the Aegean area (Cumae and Sinope; founded c.750) were halfway houses on the way to the newly discovered Tuscan and Transcaucasian mines. This mercantile pattern of colonization was soon obscured by a much more intensive programme dictated by pressure of numbers at home. Unrelated to the possibilities of trade except in so far as the colonizers favoured already explored directions, this resulted in the suitable stretches of coast nearest Greece – the sole of Italy, the east or Sicily, the Thracian Bosporus – receiving numerous foundations. In contrast to Phoenician merchant venturing, which accidentally created a new nation, Greek colonization was a deliberate extension of the existing Greek world.

At the end of the ninth century, the Dorian state of Sparta (the south-east quarter of the Peloponnese) was the subject of a peculiar and far reaching social reorganization, in which the individual was dedicated to the state and virtues almost exclusively military. In the second half of the eighth century, a long war won Sparta Messene (the south-west quarter) and completed the evolution of the Dorian tactical machine, the phalanx of armoured spearmen (hoplites). In the east, the Greeks of Cyprus had been paying tribute to the Assyrians since the time of Tiglath-Pileser III; among the dozen cities contributing are an eteoCypriote survivor and a new Phoenician colony, the rest being Greek.

In Catalonia, the Iberians were overrun by *Urnfield* Celts about 700; in the south of the peninsula contact with the Phoenicians and realization of the local mineral wealth resulted in the appearance of the only native political unit ever to be of consequence, the Kingdom of Tartessus. In Arabia, two kingdoms – Maan and Sheba – arose in the Yemen at the end of the eighth century; at the end of the fifth two more – Qataban and Hadramaut – appear on the south coast.

---

1. The first King of Nubia known to us dates from *c*.750. He initiated the conquest of Egypt, which was completed by his son; up-river the frontier was advanced beyond the confluence of the White and Blue Niles. The origins of the kingdom and dynasty are obscure, but probably both derive from the Egyptian vice-royalty; certainly the capital was at Napata, as in the days of Egyptian rule, and the panoply of government, Egyptian to the last detail.

2. In western Anatolia the Phrygian paramountcy was inherited by the Lydians, who managed to hold off the Cimmerians; the first Lydian Kings called on the Assyrians for aid, so their situation must have been precarious.

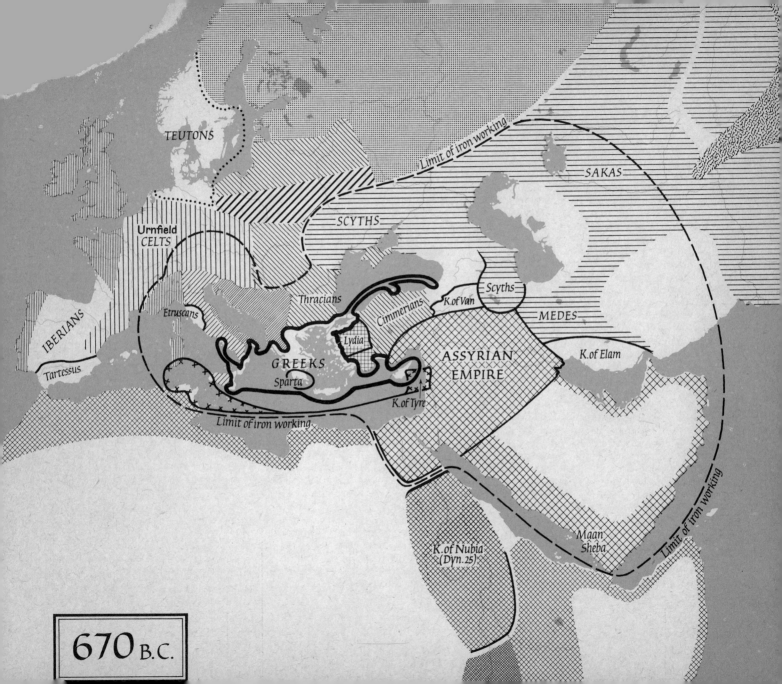

TEUTONS

Urnfield
CELTS

IBERIANS

Tartessus

Etruscans

Thracians

GREEKS

Sparta

Lydia

Cimmerians

K. of Tyre

SCYTHS

Limit of iron working

SAKAS

Scyths

K. of Van

MEDES

K. of Elam

ASSYRIAN
EMPIRE

Limit of iron working

K. of Nubia
(Dyn. 25)

Maan
Sheba

Limit of iron working

670 B.C.

The continual revolts that plagued the Assyrian Empire imply a harshness that the inscriptions of their monarchs amply confirm: they habitually make a boast of terrorism. Considering the over-extension of Assyrian resources, this seems short-sighted as well as unattractive. Impending exhaustion was apparent in the withdrawal of the Assyrian garrison from Egypt, and though Assurbanipal, the last major Assyrian king (668–626), was able to conquer and annex nearer Elam (646), the most important consequence of his campaign was that further Elam fell to the Iranian dynasty of the Achaemenids. This completed the elimination of the south-eastern Caucasians. The Iranians now held nearly all Iran, and after the defeat of the Scyths by the Median King Cyaxares the Medes held the leadership of the Iranians. This was power on the Assyrian scale, and, when Cyaxares formed an alliance with the Babylonians, who had revolted against Assyria in 625, the Assyrian armies were unable to enforce the submission of either. For a decade the war dragged on; then the Scyths went over to the allies and the balance tipped in their favour. In 612 they sacked and razed Nineveh. Pharaoh Necho (626–605), seeing a splendid opportunity to regain Egypt's ancient empire in Syria and Palestine and a perfect buffer for these provinces in a dependent Assyria, marched north to the support of a remnant Assyrian principality at Harran, but the town had fallen before he arrived (609). For a few years Necho made the Euphrates his frontier; then his complete defeat at the hands of Nebuchadnezzar of Babylon (Carchemish, 605) put an end to the possibility of either an Assyrian or an Egyptian renaissance.[1] The Transcaucasian Scyths rejoined their brethren on the Russian steppe, Nebuchadnezzar took over the fertile crescent,[2] while Cyaxares moved west. He conquered the Van region (c.595) just after the Caucasian kingdom had been finally overthrown and the country settled by the Thraco-Cimmerian people who later became known as Armenians, but in Anatolia he was held by the Lydians (c.585). Between them the Medes and Lydians had now absorbed the Phrygian and Cimmerian peoples; a fragment of the Cimmerian nation, a tribe called the Tauri, survived in the Crimea.

Sites suitable for Greek colonization were now becoming hard to find; Massilia in southern France, Cyrene in Libya and the various foundations on the north coast of the Black Sea, were the last seeds to fall on ground that was both fertile and unbroken. Massilia succeeded in establishing trading relations with Tartessus, but this success stimulated the Phoenicians of the west to form a league under Carthaginian leadership to protect their monopoly of Spanish minerals (Tyrian suzerainty was now entirely nominal), and Greek weakness soon encouraged Carthage into taking the offensive. In the east the rising power of Lydia was an even more immediate threat to Greek freedom; shortly after the date of this map, Croesus, Lydia's last and greatest king, subdued Ionia *in toto*. The metropolitan Greeks lacked the political organization that might have enabled them to support their overseas compatriots. Their strongest city, Corinth, was concerned only with commerce; their strongest league, the Thessalian (Amphictyonic), was strictly limited in scope and, like Sparta, uninterested in events outside the peninsula.

About 600, the *Urnfield* Celts entered the first (*Hallstatt*) stage of their characteristic Iron Age culture. Early on in this phase they overran the central plateau of Spain, but, as the Iberians of Catalonia simultaneously regained their independence, the invaders were cut off from their kin in France. It was probably in the seventh century that Buddha began his teaching in the Hindu principalities of the upper Ganges; Zoroaster is thought to have lived in the Oxus region towards the end of the same century.

1. Necho was the second pharaoh of the twenty-sixth dynasty. The first, originally a puppet of the Assyrians, had cleared the Nubians out of upper Egypt; he and his successors brought better government to Egypt than it had known since the days of the nineteenth dynasty so the Egyptian revival was not entirely frustrated. About the date of this map, Cyprus and Cyrene became tributary.

The Nubian kings continued to rule the Nile from the lower reaches of the White and Blue branches to the second cataract. In 591, when the Egyptians sent a punitive expedition that sacked Napata, the capital was moved upstream and out of reach to Meroe.

2. Judah got it both coming and going; its army was annihilated by Necho on his way north and Jerusalem taken by Nebuchadnezzar on his way south (597). Ten years later an Egyptian-inspired revolt led to Nebuchadnezzar's return, a second capture of the city and the deportation of the two tribes of Judah (586).

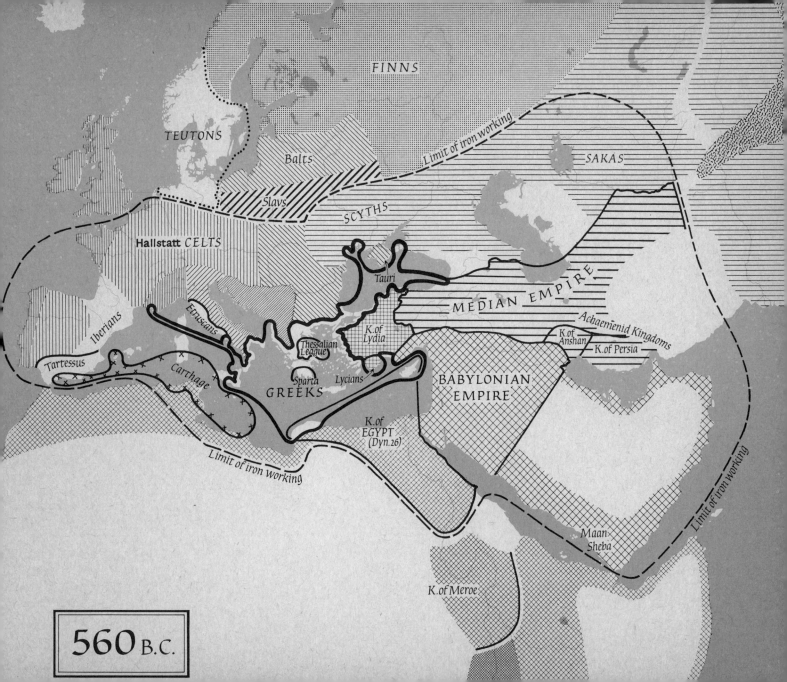

FINNS

TEUTONS

Balts

SAKAS

Slavs

*Limit of iron working*

Hallstatt CELTS

SCYTHS

Tauri

MEDIAN EMPIRE

Iberians

Etruscans

K. of
Lydia

Achaemenid Kingdoms

K. of
Anshan

Tartessus

Thessalian
League

K. of Persia

Carthage

Sparta

Lycians

BABYLONIAN
EMPIRE

GREEKS

K. of
EGYPT
(Dyn. 26)

*Limit of iron Working*

*Limit of iron working*

Maan
Sheba

K. of Meroe

560 B.C.

In 559 Cyrus II succeeded to the throne of Anshan, the senior of the two Achaemenid principalities which had replaced eastern Elam (the other being Persia); he rounded off his kingdom by taking western Elam from the Babylonians (556); seven years later he slew his Median overlord and took his place at the head of what had long been the most powerful nation in Asia. Thereafter this power was manifest. Assyria was taken from the Babylonians (548–7); a single campaign the next year sufficed for the overthrow of Croesus and the annexation of Lydia (including its Ionian Greek dependencies); a decade later came the almost bloodless conquest of the neo-Babylonian empire (539) which had been fatally weakened by the religious strife, of which a distorted memory remains in the book of Daniel.[1] In the interval, other campaigns had carried the eastern frontier to the Jaxartes. After Cyrus' death in a minor war with a Saka tribe (529) his son Cambyses II (529–2) conquered Egypt (525) and received the submission of Cyrene and Cyprus. Having achieved in two generations the natural boundaries of a world empire, the Achaemenids might have exercised a well-earned right to decline but there followed a usurpation involving some intemperately fresh blood. Darius the Persian (522–486) sought equal lustre for the junior Achaemenid line. To the east he completed, if he did not initiate, the conquest of the Indus valley (c.520);[2] in the west he crossed to Europe and marched against the Scyths (516). This last aggression was a failure which so shook Persian reputation that the Ionian Greeks risked revolt (499). Darius put them down (by 494), and despatched a small sea-borne expedition to punish the mainland Greek cities that had aided the rebels. The defeat of this force by the Athenians at Marathon (491) is writ large in Greek history but it was only the opening skirmish in a war to which the prestige-conscious

50

Darius felt he must now commit himself. He died before his preparations were complete and it was his son Xerxes (486–465) who led against the Greeks the famous host which, if not to be numbered in the millions of later oratory, was certainly incomparably larger than any hitherto seen in Europe.[3] Macedon and Thessaly fell without a struggle but some sharp fighting had to be done before the pass of Thermopylae could be cleared and Athens occupied (480). There remained only the Spartan army and the Athenian fleet.

Pressure on the western Greeks was almost as severe, following the formation of an anti-Greek front by the Carthaginians and Etruscans. The Etruscans were now at the height of their power, having expanded into the Po valley and down the western coast of Italy to Campania.[4] In 535 the Carthaginians and Etruscans together forced the Greeks to withdraw from Corsica (which passed to the Etruscans) and c.510 the Carthaginians' conquest of Tartessus resulted in the exclusion of Massiliote traders from the southern part of the peninsula. The success of their enterprises encouraged the Carthaginians to carry them to a conclusion; in 481 a Carthaginian army was landed on Sicily, the reduction of the whole island its avowed aim.

A new fashion of decorating urns with faces replaced the *Lausitz* style within the Slav zone about this date. The change is said to spread south-eastwards from the Baltic, and on this basis German scholars have held that their ancestors were ordering Slavs about as early as the fifth century: there is, however, nothing to suggest any Teutonic expansion at this time and the technological backwardness of the area makes it unlikely. The Bastarnae, who have been cast as the heroes of this imaginary saga, were Celts.[5]

To this era date the beginnings of a cross-channel movement to England by *Hallstatt* Celts, and of South Arabian colonization of the Eritrean coast. On the Russian steppe the Iranian tribes between the Don and the Aral become known as Sarmatians, as against the Scyths to their west and the Sakas to the east.

1. After the fall of Babylon, the two tribes of Judah returned to Jerusalem with Cyrus' blessing.
2. This almost completely undocumented advance is of great importance to Indian history for it marks the introduction into the sub-continent of coinage, iron working and writing. With the start of iron working in Britain, Scandinavia and India (and also, incidentally, in China) there is no further need for the line showing the geographical limits of this technique. Negro Africa remained without useful metals until the first century B.C. when iron working began in the Niger basin: its further spread was also slow, the East African Iron Age only beginning c.750–1000 A.D.
3. It has been suggested that Xerxes took with him half the Empire's total levy of 360,000 men.
4. The Etruscans provided kings for the Italic town of Rome c.550–475 (traditionally 616–509).
5. See page 72, note 3.

FINNS

SAKAS

TEUTONS

Balts

SARMATIANS

Slavs

SCYTHS

Hallstatt CELTS

PERSIAN EMPIRE

Massilia

Etruscans

CARTHAGE

Spartan League
GREEKS

Maan
Sheba

K.of Meroe

480 B.C.

Xerxes could not force the Corinthian isthmus and complete the conquest of Greece until he had destroyed the Athenian fleet, and after his attempt to do so had resulted in the destruction of his own (Salamis, 480) he had perforce to abandon the offensive. He returned home leaving half the expeditionary force to garrison Attica. Next year the Spartan hoplites debouched from the Peloponnese and the Persian army of occupation shattered at their first blundering contact (Plataea, 479). The Greeks of Sicily were as dramatically delivered, the Carthaginians going down before the Syracusans at the battle of Himera in the same year as Salamis – later historians improved this to the same day.

Once the Persians had been defeated, the Spartan horizon again contracted to the coast line of the Peloponnese, and it was left to Athens to exploit the Greek military superiority that the war had revealed. Immediately after the battle the Athenian fleet seized the Hellespont, cutting off the Persians in Macedonia and Thrace and re-opening the Black Sea to Greek shipping; then, in a series of campaigns spread over the next few years, the Athenians proceeded to liberate the northern and eastern shores of the Aegean. But the towns and islands were freed only to be enrolled in an anti-Persian league in which Athens had the decisive voice, and they soon found that the helping hand rested on their shoulders with a weight reminiscent of the Persian. As the essentially maritime power of the league could hardly challenge Persian control of the Anatolian interior, the original purpose of the association was fulfilled with the recapture of Ionia, and its continuation demanded and received a new dedication: to Aegean peace and the expansion of trade. So strict was the control that Athens exerted over the league and so complete was her grip on all profit-earning activities that she soon came to regard her allies as possessions and the league as her empire. The extension of this domineering attitude to the states of peninsular Greece finally brought her into conflict with the Spartans who, if politically lethargic, were strongly conscious of their traditional primacy and were not prepared to tolerate indefinitely the repeated needling of the greedy, cocksure Athenians.

The result of the first (457–451) of the four wars between the two was a sharp defeat for Athens after which she wisely abandoned the minor local ambitions which had precipitated it. But, when she turned her attention overseas again, she looked westward, along the rich trade routes to southern Italy and Sicily, and her moves in this direction antagonized the city that dominated this traffic, Corinth. As Corinth was a member of the Spartan league, Sparta was soon involved, and, while the second war (431–421) was a fish and fox contest that could have no end but a draw, the third (413–404) saw a Spartan fleet, paid for by the Persians, take the sea and destroy the delicate structure of the Athenian league. But when Sparta seemed disposed to revive the anti-Persian crusade, Persian subsidies were re-routed to Athens and Thebes. Sparta regained Persian favour by ceding Ionia (387) but could not prevent the creation of a new Athenian league (this time minus Ionia and also the Crimean Bosporus, since 438 an independent kingdom[1]) in a desultory fourth war that betrayed the exhaustion and political impotence of the contestants.

Persian diplomacy and Persian gold had brought the Greek counter-offensive to a halt. Elsewhere the Empire was losing ground: Egypt revolted successfully c.400 (under the short-lived twenty-eighth, twenty-ninth and thirtieth native dynasties) and the Indian provinces fell away c.380.

That the Carthaginians long accepted the verdict of Himera, refraining from further attempts on Sicily until the end of the fifth century, was probably a consequence of the rapid decline of their Etruscan allies. About 475 the Syracusans drove the Etruscans from Campanian waters and the Latins, under the leadership of Rome, successfully repudiated Etruscan suzerainty. Syracuse was able to maintain the hegemony over the turbulent Sicilian Greeks, extend it over the tribes of the interior (c.410) and beat off a gratuitous Athenian attack (415–413), all without Carthaginian interference. But finally Greek raids on the west of the island provoked the unaggressive Carthaginians to a punitive expedition (409) and its unexpectedly easy success encouraged them to attempt the conquest of the island again. In 406 the Carthaginians destroyed Acragas, and Syracusan hegemony in the island vanished as a result of successive defeats. Syracuse herself held out, however, and, as the fighting became more indecisive and the prospect of complete success receded, the Carthaginians' appetite dwindled. The peace treaty of 392 restored the pre-war frontiers, and Syracuse returned to her old position as protector and master of the western Greeks. Warned by the fate of Capua and Cumae which had fallen to the Italic Samnites (423, 420), the southern Italian cities took shelter under her mantle, but the Athens of the West extracted as high a tribute from her subjects as did Athens herself. Her aims were selfish, her rule tyrannical, her performance hair-raisingly erratic.

In Europe the main feature of the period was the evolution of a new culture (*La Tene*) in the old Celtic homelands, which marks the appearance in history of the Gauls and the beginning of the second phase of P-Celtic expansion. Pressure down the Danube probably began at this time; the invasion of Italy, with the obliteration of the Etruscan colonies in the Po valley and the trans-Apennine raid that culminated in the sack of Rome, can be fixed more exactly to the period 410–390.

1. The title of king was not actually used till 309. The ruling dynasty was Tauric by blood but Greek in manner.

TEUTONS

Sakas

Sarmatians

Scyths

Hallstatt CELTS

GAULS
(La Tene CELTS)

K.of
Macedon

Bosporan K.

PERSIAN EMPIRE

Massilia    Etruscans

Latin League

CARTHAGE

Syracuse

Athens

Sparta
GREEKS

K.of
Egypt
(Dyn.30)

Hadramaut

Maan
Sheba    Qataban

K.of Meroe

375 B.C.

'The Lydians were the first nation to introduce the use of gold and silver coins, and the first who sold goods by retail.' So says Herodotus; and as for a century or more before the first issue of gold and silver coins (by Croesus, 550) the Lydians had had a currency of hallmarked electrum slugs[1] the beginnings of the market economy can be put back to about 700. Living in that artificial construct, a free society, and regarding the regulation of price by supply and demand as something akin to a natural law, it is difficult for us to visualize the economic processes of primitive communities. Their essential feature is a sort of rationing system that is not egalitarian but hierarchical; you are allowed three strings of beads if and when you are entitled to wear them. Consumption is both conspicuous and mandatory and its primary purpose is to express rank. The Communists have partly reverted to this system in protest at the destructive social effects of *laissez-faire* economics, but the price of re-tribalization is liberty. Conversely, the liberation of the individual from the social mould was the dynamic behind the seventh century upsurge of the Aegean peoples. In contrast to the towns of Mesopotamia which had no market places (Herodotus again, confirmed by archaeology), the agora was the recognized centre of the Greek city. With a fistful of coins and an eye for the main chance, the individual had arrived in history.

The search for a social system to match the new-style economy, counter its divisive effects and translate economic into political power, was to be a long and painful process for the Greeks. The initial, colonizing phase of their expansion, an overflow that was successful only where it was unopposed, won few primary resources. The fisheries and wheat fields of the Black Sea colonies answered some of the needs of the over-populated homeland; elsewhere, the Greeks were trading with foreigners whose enmity, understandably enough in view of frequent if ineffectual Greek grabs at their property, only occasionally softened to suspicion. The Greeks traded their wine, oil and manufactures (mostly pottery) for Carthaginian (Spanish) and Etruscan metals and the traditional products of Egypt and the East.

The node of the Greek trading network lay at the Peloponnesian isthmus, where goods were easily trans-shipped or, especially after 600 when a paved way was built, the ships themselves could be hauled across. The first major town in Greece was the isthmian capital, Corinth; her wares were the staple of the pottery trade until the rise of Athens and she continued to dominate the routes to the West even after this. What Corinth owed to position, Athens owed to the discovery of silver at nearby Laurion (c.550). This paid for the navy which triumphed at Salamis, liberated the Ionians, collected their tribute and guaranteed safe passage to the grain ships from the Black Sea on which the existence of the enlarged city came to depend. On land Athens was never strong enough to protect her farmers whose concentration on the cash crops of the Mediterranean world, wine and oil, was not so imprudent as appears at first sight; the walls of the city could resist any assault and while the Athenian navy ruled the waves the grain supply was assured and the cheaper for being imported. Cypriot and Egyptian revolts against Persian rule gave opportunities for economic penetration of the Levant;[2] Tyre, in decline since Carthage and the route to Spain had slipped from her control, suffered repeated defeat in the Persian cause and dwindled to a city of the second rank.[3] In the horizontal division of the Mediterranean into Carthaginian and Greek spheres, she became a cipher and, when the Athenian grip on the Aegean was finally broken, the beneficiary was not Tyre but Rhodes. By the second half of the fourth century Rhodes had the major share of the traffic in the Black Sea, Aegean and Levant. By then the mines of Laurion were exhausted; their place in the Greek economy was taken by the alluvial deposits in the north which were worked to the profit of Philip of Macedon.

The attentions that the Greeks and Carthaginians paid to the mineral-rich parts of Spain and Italy early stimulated the natives into political consciousness. The kingdom of Tartessus was overwhelmed in its infancy, but the Etruscans and Italics withstood the newcomers and developed a city-centred way of life in imitation of the Greek. Etruscan towns always remained small – in the 5–10,000 population bracket – but by the early fourth century Rome must have passed the 10,000 mark and drawn level with Tarentum, the largest Greek city in Italy. The hinterland of Europe remained largely unaffected; when the backdoor attempt on Spain failed, the Massiliotes found a limited compensation in trade with the Gauls (some British tin reached the Mediterranean this way) and there was also contact with the Celts of Germany via the Adriatic. A formal amber route can be allowed at this date and Bohemian tin accepted as one of its most important commodities (amber was out of fashion in Greece); however, it was the Etruscan colonies in the Po valley that had originally attracted Greek interest, and, after their overthrow, Adriatic traffic was never of much importance.

Apart from Babylon the city of the first rank (30,000 or more inhabitants) is now a Mediterranean phenomenon; reversing the previous position its prosperity has become more commercial than imperial. The Persians, a pastoral people, failed to promote the urban life of the Near East or even to sustain it at the Assyrian level. They did, however, bring Egypt out of economic isolation and incidentally completed the Nile–Red Sea canal begun by Necho.

1. Electrum is a gold-silver alloy that occurs naturally in Anatolia.
2. The western situation of the new capital, Sais, marks the shift in Egypt's orientation.
3. The Tyrians (and Carthaginians) clung to the system of community trading; their coinage only starts in the fourth century.

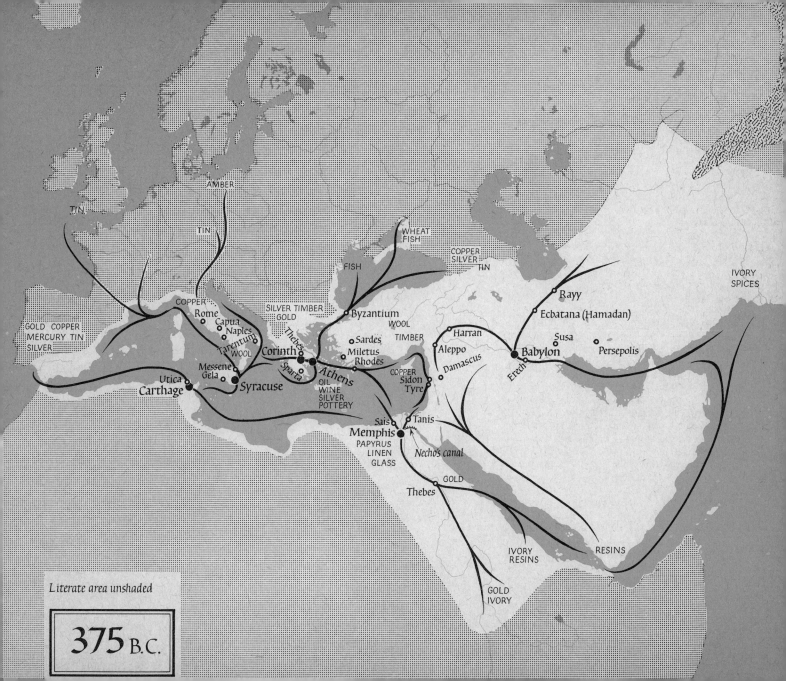

TIN

AMBER

TIN

WHEAT
FISH

COPPER
SILVER
TIN

IVORY
SPICES

FISH

Rayy

Ecbatana (Hamadan)

COPPER

GOLD COPPER
MERCURY TIN
SILVER

SILVER TIMBER
GOLD

Byzantium

WOOL

Susa

Rome

Sardes

TIMBER

Harran

Babylon

Persepolis

Capua
Naples

Thebes

Aleppo

Tarentum

WOOL

Corinth

Miletus
Rhodes

Damascus

Erech

Messene
Gela

Sparta

Athens

COPPER

Utica

Syracuse

OIL
WINE
SILVER
POTTERY

Sidon
Tyre

Carthage

Sais

Tanis

Memphis

PAPYRUS
LINEN
GLASS

Necho's canal

Thebes

GOLD

IVORY
RESINS

RESINS

GOLD
IVORY

Literate area unshaded

**375** B.C.

Most of the credit for the increase in size of the literate zone since 825 and entire responsibility for improvement in technique during this period belongs to the Greeks. Around 800, they adopted the Phoenician consonantal alphabet; five letters that were superfluous to Greek consonantal requirements were used to represent vowels. The use of vowel-signs marks the appearance of the true alphabet. Phrygian, Lydian, Carian and Lycian alphabets appear in the Aegean area immediately after this, as do Etruscan and Illyrian alphabets shortly after the arrival of the Greeks in the Italian peninsula. From Etruscan were derived the Italic alphabets including the Latin. The literacy of the Mediterranean was eventually completed when the Libyans and Iberians borrowed the Phoenician letters from the Carthaginians.

For administrative purposes, the Persians used the Aramaic language and writing; the surviving Persian-language inscriptions are in a cuneiform script which is half alphabet, half open syllabary. This was probably reserved for monumental use and it is thought that day to day Persian correspondence was already being written in an Aramaic-derived script ancestral to the Pahlavi of the Parthian period. The Indians evolved two alphabets from the Aramaic; the earlier Brahmi script as a result of spice route contacts; the Kharoshthi script as a result of the Persian conquest of the Indus valley.

Elamite and Babylonian cuneiform, the Cypriot syllabary and Egyptian hieroglyphic continued in local use.

Palaeographical theories depend on the accidents of archaeological discovery and recently Phrygian alphabetic inscriptions have been discovered that are as old as the earliest Greek examples. Could the invention of vowel-signs be Phrygian and not Greek? The Greeks believed that they had evolved their alphabet directly from Phoenician, and scholars have always believed the Greeks: but the possibility that the transmission was overland and the introduction of vowel-signs an Anatolian achievement cannot be ignored.

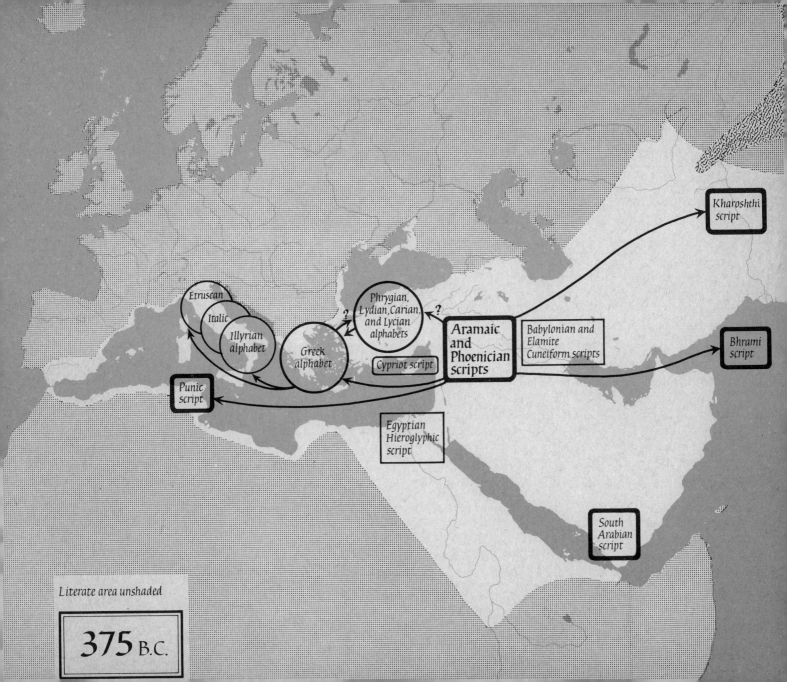

Kharoshthi script

Etruscan

Italic

Illyrian alphabet

Phrygian, Lydian, Carian, and Lycian alphabets

? ?

Aramaic and Phoenician scripts

Babylonian and Elamite Cuneiform scripts

Bhrami script

Greek alphabet

Cypriot script

Punic script

Egyptian Hieroglyphic script

South Arabian script

Literate area unshaded

375 B.C.

In the opening years of his reign, Philip II, King of Macedon (359–336), transformed the levy of his backwoods state into the largest and most efficient force in Greece.[1] The discovery of gold deposits permitted the increase in size; the increase in efficiency stemmed from Philip's refusal to accept two conventions of Greek warfare that were responsible for its typically indecisive quality: the restriction of campaigning to a recognized season and of seige technique to blockade. Thracians and Illyrians provided Philip with an inexhaustible supply of enemies and he fought them the year round; cities that defied him he assaulted, often with success. As early as 352, when he annexed Thessaly, the established powers of Greece had their warning; but intent on a squabble over the sanctuary of Delphi – they called it the Sacred War – they put off forming an anti-Macedonian coalition until the last possible moment. By then (338), Philip was unstoppable. The combined Theban–Athenian army was crushed at the battle of Chaeronea and the states of Greece forcibly enrolled in a pan-Hellenic league that took its orders from Philip.[2]

One of Philip's first announcements to the league proclaimed a crusade against Persia. Far from being a mere propaganda move to justify tyranny at home, this was a genuine statement of intention, underlined by extensive recruiting. By regaining possession of Egypt, the Persians had restored the perimeter of their empire, but as for a century now they had been relying on Greek mercenaries to do their fighting for them, Philip, with the best army in Greece, had sound reasons for confidence. His assassination (inspired either by the Persians or by his colourful Epirote wife, Olympias) left his son Alexander with an expeditionary force that only an empire of Persian size could afford to pay. After two quick campaigns to overawe the Greeks and Thracians (during the

first he razed Thebes, during the second he established friendly relations with the Gauls of the middle Danube), he crossed to Asia. His first victory, the rout of a Persian army that attempted to hold him at the river Granicus, gained him Anatolia and relieved him of his most pressing financial worries.[3] After organizing this conquest – the Ionian cities were 'liberated' (that is enrolled in a tax-free but politically impotent league) but otherwise the Persian system of satraps (governors) was retained – Alexander crossed the Taurus, defeated the main Persian army at Issus and occupied Syria, Palestine and Egypt. The Persians sent a peace offer based on the *status quo* which Philip would surely have accepted; Alexander, conscious of his destiny, marched on. In the battle of Arbela he destroyed the last Persian army and won the empire; then he disappeared beyond the Greek horizon, spending the last years of his brief life in minor campaigns on, or, in the case of India, beyond the ancient Persian frontier. His army needed only competent leadership to win its set-piece battles, and it was in the conduct of such secondary operations that Alexander's genius was tested and triumphed. In inexorable succession citadels were scaled, hill tribes were ambushed and the horsemen of the steppe out-run. In India it took a sit-down strike of his soldiers to prevent him advancing to the Ganges; in his last days he was planning the circumnavigation and conquest of Arabia; but in seeking fresh worlds to conquer he neglected the completion of his colossal achievement. The native rulers of the satrapies of Bithynia, Cappadocia and Armenia (superficially Iranised but basically Phrygian) and of Atropatene (Median) were left undisturbed after they had rendered the most perfunctory homage; worse still, the heirs to his empire were a feeble-minded brother and a posthumous son.

While the Etruscans never really recovered from the onslaught of the Gauls, Rome not only beat back the invaders but imposed on the confederate Latins a discipline so severe that by 338

her original primacy in the league had become absolute rule. The conquest of Campania (341) was the first sign that here was the strongest power in Italy.

1. At Athens it was fashionable to affect difficulty in distinguishing the Macedonians from their barbarian (non-Greek) neighbours and Athenophile historians have been apt to take this bit of snobbery literally. Grote, for example, remarks in a sniffy aside that there were more Greeks in the army of the Persians than in that of Alexander. Putting the Macedonians in the same category as, say, the Epirotes (a people of admittedly barbarian, in this case Illyrian, blood whose Hellenized upper classes passed as Greek) is certainly wrong; not only were they indubitably Greek, but they Hellenized more than their fair share of barbarians – including the Epirotes, whose monarchy was created by Philip as part of his programme for pacifying and controlling the borderlands.

2. Sparta stayed out of the league and was not compelled to join until 331, when she made an unsuccessful attack on Alexander's viceroy.

3. There was still insufficient money to pay for a fleet and a Phoenician squadron operating in the Aegean caused some worrying moments. The occupation of the Phoenician coastline the next year put an end to this problem.

TEUTONS

Sakas

Sarmatians

Scyths

GAULS
(La Tene CELTS)

Bosporan K.

K. of
Bithynia

S. of
Cappadocia

S. of Armenia

S. of Atropatene

K. of
Porus

Massilia    Etruscans   Rome

Ionia

Hellenic
League

Syracuse

Epirus

CARTHAGE

EMPIRE OF ALEXANDER

Hadramaut

Maan
Sheba    Qataban

K. of Meroe

323 B.C.

Although for a few years after Alexander's death a central authority was maintained, lack of a capable royal successor made it inevitable that power would devolve on the generals in the provinces. In little more than a decade generals had become kings: Cassander in Macedon, Lysimachus in Thrace, Antigonus in Anatolia and Syria, Ptolemy in Egypt and Seleucus in the East. Of them all, only the seventy-year-old Antigonus had the will to restore the unity of the Empire. Though he had the advantages of central position and command of the sea and by clever propaganda was able to seduce the Hellenic league from its allegiance to Cassander,[1] his failure to disguise his ultimate ambition caused his enemies to combine against him. The old man went down fighting before the united armies of Cassander, Lysimachus and Seleucus in the critical battle of Ipsus (301). Seleucus took Syria and Cilicia, and Lysimachus Anatolia, while Ptolemy, who in his careful way had been too late for the battle, obtained Palestine and Cyprus. Though Antigonus' son Demetrius had escaped to his fleet and was to be heard from again, he had only the resources – and mentality – of a freebooter. The imperial idea was dead.

Cappadocia had been brought under Macedonian control in the immediate post-Alexander period; thereafter the successor kings made little effort to enlarge their dominions except at each other's expense.[2] In the turmoil, outlying satrapies such as Armenia, Atropatene and, after Ipsus, Pontic Cappadocia,[3] became independent. Seleucus gracefully evacuated the untenable Indian provinces on which Alexander had lavished so much of his skill; they went to swell the empire of Chandragupta, the founder of the Maurya dynasty, whose dominion had now spread from the ancient centres of Hindu power in the Ganges valley across the whole north of the sub-continent.

While Greek attention was concentrated on the exploitation of the East, the position of the western colonists was deteriorating. Carthage forced the Massiliotes back along the coast of Spain, took over Corsica and, in 311, conquered all Sicily bar Syracuse. Though, thanks to a brilliantly conceived counter-blow at Carthage, the Syracusans were able to obtain the restitution of Greek Sicily (306) the struggle was clearly becoming unequal. This was even more true of Italy where the Greeks had never been able to do much more than keep the local tribes at bay and where the accelerating advance of Roman power carried a challenge that they could not hope to meet. In some of the local wars Tarentum, the leading city of southern Italy, had employed Epirote and Spartan *condottieri*; the need now was for an Alexander.

1. Antigonus brought Ionia under direct rule and promoted a new league for the islands. Rhodes was strong enough to ignore it.

2. The few attempts they did make are worth a brief mention: Cassander momentarily pushed westward to the Adriatic; Lysimachus conquered Thrace as far as the Danube and imposed himself on the towns of the Thracian Black Sea coast but ignominiously failed in an attempt to extend across the river; Antigonus made an unsuccessful grab at Petra, the capital of the Nabataean Arabs of southern Palestine.

3. The maritime province of Cappadocia, from now on known as Pontus; it first appears on the next map.

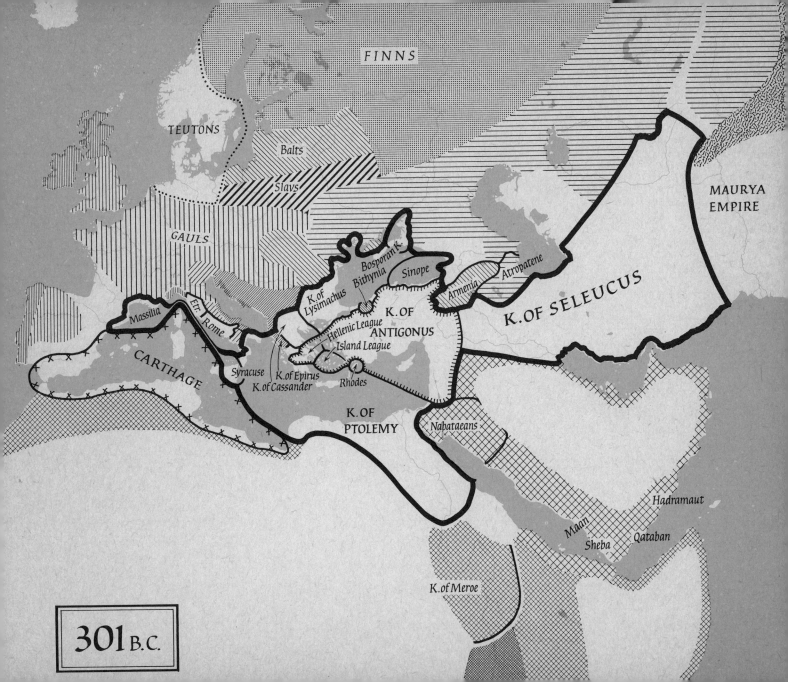

FINNS

TEUTONS

Balts

Slavs

GAULS

MAURYA
EMPIRE

K. of
Lysimachus

Bosporan K.
Bithynia

Sinope

Armenia

Atropatene

Massilia

Etr. Rome

K. OF
ANTIGONUS

K. OF SELEUCUS

CARTHAGE

Syracuse

Hellenic League

Island League

K. of Epirus
K. of Cassander

Rhodes

K. OF
PTOLEMY

Nabataeans

Hadramaut

Maan

Sheba

Qataban

K. of Meroe

301 B.C.

The battle of Ipsus did not put an end to the struggles of Alexander's successors. By virtue of his fleet Demetrius was able to control the Aegean and much of mainland Greece and shortly after Cassander's death he seized Macedon (298). Lysimachus soon forced him out again, his fleet deserted to Ptolemy and, after a last wandering campaign in Anatolia, he ended up a prisoner of Seleucus. Lysimachus was the next to go, killed in battle by Seleucus at Corupedium in Ionia (280). Macedon and the mantle of Alexander his for the taking, Seleucus crossed to Europe, only to be assassinated as he stepped out of the boat. And then from the north came the Gauls, pouring into Macedon, peninsular Greece and Thrace (279). Demetrius' son, Antigonus II, cleaned them out of Macedon and seized the throne (which was to remain in his house thereafter), but in Thrace the invaders founded a robber kingdom, and three tribes crossed the Hellespont and established themselves permanently in the central region of Anatolia – from now on known as Galatia. These Gauls, who intermittently plundered Anatolia throughout the third century, effectively screened the native kingdoms of Bithynia and Pontus from Seleucid interference. The political fragmentation of Asia Minor was carried a stage further when Ptolemy II used his sea-power to relieve Antiochus, Seleucus' son and heir, of much of his western seaboard. Ptolemy's new-found fleet dominated the Aegean, so in the event of trouble with either of his rivals it was an easy matter for him to raise Greece against Antigonus or Ionia against Antiochus. However, though trouble remained endemic, a balance had at last been struck and the successor states had assumed their definitive form.

To champion the cause of Hellenism against the Romans the Tarentines picked Pyrrhus, King of Epirus, who was always game for a war. He arrived in Italy in 281 with a large army and larger ambitions. Unfortunately for him the opportune moment for intervention had passed for, in the opening decades of the century, the Romans had finally mastered their native enemies – the Etruscans, Samnites (Italics) and nearer Gauls – and, though Pyrrhus won his battles, he failed to raise the country. When, in 278, the Sicilian Greeks appealed to him for help against a new Carthaginian offensive, he preferred the chance of dramatic victories to the task of grinding down Rome's legions. His success was indeed rapid and for a moment he was able to regard Sicily as his second kingdom. The Sicilian Greeks, however, were no keener to surrender their freedom to Pyrrhus than to Carthage; they revolted and he abandoned them, as next year he abandoned the Italian Greeks for a war with Antigonus II. He overran Macedon, lost it, and was attempting the conquest of the Peloponnese when he was killed in a skirmish (272).[1] Only then could the bewildered Romans be sure they had won.

Both Macedonian control over the Hellenic league and the league itself disappeared during the wars of the successors. By garrisoning strategic points Antigonus II was able to keep a grip on the peninsula but he was never strong enough to marshall its member states into a subservient system. For a while the old pieces in the Greek war-game, Sparta and Athens, are on the board again, jostled by such newcomers as Epirus and Aetolia: where once Persia had paid, now it was Ptolemy.

1. Ambitious kings finally tried the resources of the Epirotes too far and in 231 the monarchy was overthrown.

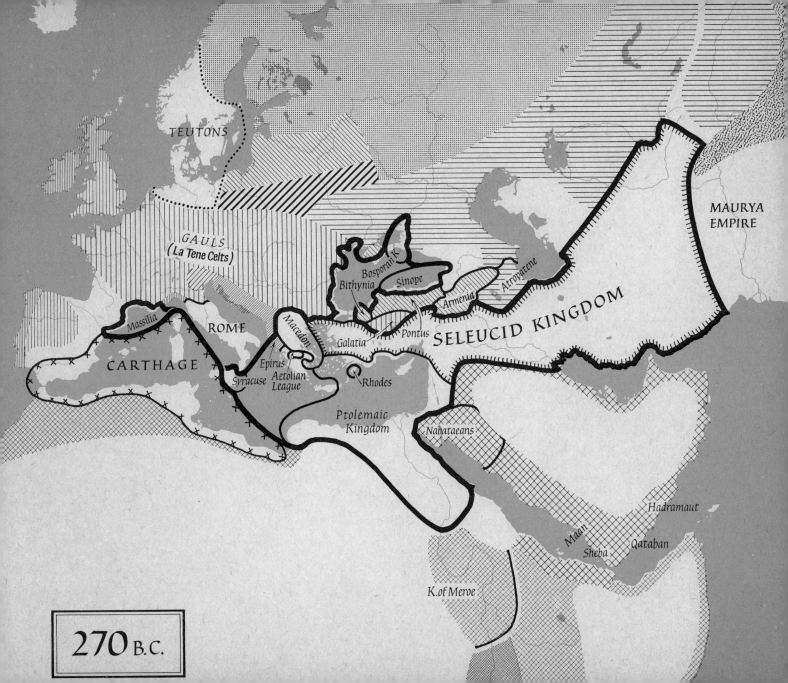

TEUTONS

GAULS
(La Tene Celts)

MASSILIA

ROME

CARTHAGE

Macedon

Epirus
Syracuse
Aetolian
League

Galatia

Bosporan K.
Bithynia
Sinope

Pontus

Armenia

Atropatene

SELEUCID KINGDOM

MAURYA
EMPIRE

Rhodes

Ptolemaic
Kingdom

Nabataeans

Hadramaut

Maon

Sheba    Qataban

K. of Meroe

270 B.C.

Italy mastered, the Romans looked to Sicily. At first Syracuse and Carthage combined against them but the Syracusans quickly changed sides and preserved a limited freedom after the Romans' final victory in what became known as the first Punic war (264–241).[1] During the desultory twenty-year struggle the Romans gradually won control over the island; but this local success was less significant than the creation of a Roman navy and the disappearance, after repeated defeats, of the Carthaginian fleet. The imperial outlook fostered by the possession of this new weapon was soon apparent. Corsica and Sardinia were lifted from Carthage (237) at a time when she was paralysed by trouble with the Berbers of the hinterland (now organizing into the kingdoms of Numidia and Mauretania); a foothold in Illyria resulted from a campaign to eliminate piracy in the Adriatic (228).

Carthage still retained control of the coast of Spain as far north as the Ebro and, as soon as order had been restored on the home front by the reduction of the Numidian kingdom to vassal status, she began to extend her authority over the Iberian, Celtic and Ligurian tribes of the Spanish interior. Years of hard campaigning brought her a continental empire richer than the thalassocracy she had lost and an army that was tougher than her navy had ever been. Her revival re-awakened the hostility of the Romans, who sent an embassy to Saguntum, an ex-ally of Massilia now in the Carthaginian sector of Spain, with a promise of support in the event of trouble with Carthage. Although the Carthaginians were far from relishing the prospect of a second trial of strength, such interference in their internal affairs was impossible to accept. Hannibal, the Carthaginian proconsul in Spain, took Saguntum by storm; the Roman delegation sent to demand his punishment returned from Carthage empty-handed.

64

Along with the greater part of Alexander's empire, the Seleucids inherited the problems he would have had to face: Greek factionalism, provincial separatism and Iranian reaction. Add the enmity of other successor-states and it is no surprise to find the Seleucid giant flabby in action. The Ptolemies soon completed their control of the coast of Greek Asia Minor, either by direct seizure or by subsidizing Pergamum (independent since 262), at once the strongest and the most anti-Seleucid of the cities of Ionia. In the interior of Anatolia the Kingdom of (inland) Cappadocia arose in independence of the Seleucids (260); in the east the Parthians (an Iranian people) and the Bactrians (Iranians under a Greek dynasty) seceded c.250. Macedon, on the other hand, gradually regained control of Greece; in 224 an obedient Hellenic league was re-established, complete except for the Athenians and Aetolians.

The Gallic tide was now ebbing: the Galatians of Anatolia were confined by the rival efforts of Seleucids and Pergamenes; the Romans completed their conquest of the Po valley (236–222) and, at the end of the century, the Thracians reasserted themselves. The only gain was in Britain where the first *La Tene* Celts arrived about this time.

Under Asoka, the Buddhists' ideal monarch, the Maurya empire reached its peak; after his death (232) the decline of the central authority into impotence and disunity was rapid; it is probable that the portion of the empire visible in this map was held by one of Asoka's sons as an independent kingdom.

In the Yemen, Sheba absorbed Maan c.250.

1. Punic, a contracted form of Phoenician, is used as a synonym for Carthaginian.

The absorption of the western Greeks by Rome was completed with the tacit admission by the Massiliotes that the Romans were their protectors in quarrels with Carthage. Though Syracuse and Massilia both retained local autonomy, Syracuse until an unsuccessful rebellion (215–211) in the second Punic war, Massilia until she picked the wrong side in the struggle between Caesar and Pompey (47), they no longer require distinguishing as political entities.

TEUTONS

Sakas

Sarmatians

K. of
Bactria

MAURYA
EMPIRE

Scyths

GAULS

Bithynia
Bosporan K.

Sinope

Armenia

Parthians

Pontus

Atropatene

ROME

Macedon
and the
Hellenic
League

Sophene

Cappadocia

SELEUCID KINGDOM

Pergamum

CARTHAGE

Aetolian
League

Athens

Rhodes

K. of
Mauretania

K. of Numidia

Ptolemaic
Kingdom

Nabataeans

Hadramaut

Sheba

Qataban

K. of Meroe

220 B.C.

Confident in their command of the sea, the Romans envisaged their second conflict with Carthage as an affair to be fought out at a safe distance from Italy, but Hannibal's gambit – a dramatic march from Spain across the south of France and over the Alps – brought the war to the Romans' doorstep. He won a neat victory in the Po valley before the end of that year (218) and in the next, after crossing the Apennines, destroyed two legions in an outsize ambush by Lake Trasimene. The Romans reacted with their usual dour vigour, sending four legions against him for the campaign of 216; in the battle of Cannae, his masterpiece, Hannibal annihilated them. For the next decade the Romans refused his offers of battle and restricted themselves to harassing him from the cities that, for lack of a siege train, he could not take. As the years passed his position gradually deteriorated, and the Romans gained the strategic initiative when they conquered Spain (210–206). In 204 a Roman army landed on Carthaginian home ground. Hannibal, blockaded into ineffectuality in the Italian toe, was recalled to Africa and finally met defeat at the battle of Zama (202); Carthage surrendered the next year. The Romans kept Spain and substantially enlarged Numidia both as a reward for her help in the last stages of the war and as a check against possible Carthaginian revival.

No sooner was the long struggle over than Rome had to turn east where, after the death of Ptolemy IV (203), Egypt had fallen into a disarray that excited Seleucid and Macedonian appetites.[1] Antiochus III (223–187) had proved his generalship by establishing Seleucid hegemony over Atropatene (220) and Armenia (212), defeating and confining the Parthians (209; they had overrun several of the eastern provinces a few years previously) and fighting the expanding state of Bactria to a standstill (208–206). He proceeded to the conquest of Palestine and southern Anatolia (201–197), while his ally, Philip V of Macedon, shattered the by now nominal suzerainty of the Ptolemies in Ionia and began the substitution of his own harsher government. The independent states of Pergamum and Rhodes appealed to Rome for protection, and, though the Senators were not overly concerned for the fate of distant Greek cities, they allowed themselves to be persuaded, quite against the evidence, that the Seleuco–Macedonian axis was aimed ultimately at Rome. Philip V had already earned their enmity by an alliance with Hannibal and an attempt on the Illyrian protectorate during the late war – countered at the time by a small expeditionary force and an alliance with the Aetolians and Pergamenes. Now the Senators despatched two legions. Philip marshalled his phalanx but the legions he had to face were immeasurably more sophisticated than those Pyrrhus had routed a century before; their superiority was decisively demonstrated on the field of Cynoscephalae (197). It was the end for the hoplite, and for the Macedonian supremacy in Greece. Contenting themselves with a slight enlargement of their Illyrian foothold, the victors blandly assured the Greeks that though they had no intention of taking Macedon's place in the peninsula, the Roman Senate's views must be respected, and, if unknown, solicited. Of course.

Antiochus, whose understanding with Philip had related to Egypt only, had meanwhile been re-asserting Seleucid rights in Ionia and Thrace. His eastern exploits had blinded his court, if not himself, to the many weaknesses of his polyglot state and led to his acclamation as a second Alexander; consequently, the sliver of Thrace that was a legitimate part of the Seleucid inheritance was interpreted by the Romans as a beachhead for the invasion of Europe. When Hannibal appeared in Antiochus' train, the Senate, egged on by Pergamum,[2] decided to go to war with the King (192). Antiochus quickly took up an offer from the Aetolians, who were disgruntled with the meagre rewards of the Roman alliance, and shipped an army to Greece late the same year.

On the Russian steppe the Sarmatians disposed of the Scyths, driving the defeated remnants into the Danube delta and the Crimea (the Tauri disappear). This upheaval perhaps provoked the northward advance of the middle Dneiper Slavs who, over the next century or so, ejected or absorbed the Balts of the upper Dneiper basin.

---

1. The Nubians of Meroe also advanced their frontier at Egypt's expense from the second cataract to a point not far south of the first.

2. Antiochus had temporarily placated Rhodes by granting her the coastline of Caria which had been among his conquests from Ptolemy in 197, but Rhodes joined his enemies immediately war broke out.

TEUTONS

GAULS

Sarmatians

Scyths

Sakas

K. of
Bactria

Parthians

ROME

Macedon

Bosporan K.
Bithynia
Sinope
Pontus

Armenia
Atropatene

Sophene

SELEUCID KINGDOM

Aetolian
League

Pergamum

Cappadocia

Rhodes

K. of
Mauretania

K. of Numidia

Carthage

Ptolemaic
Kingdom

Nabataeans

Hadramaut

Maan
Sheba
Qataban

K. of Meroe

**192** B.C.

The Romans quickly pushed Antiochus out of Greece and, crossing to Asia Minor, routed his forces in a battle near Magnesia (190). Once again Rome took nothing for herself, merely aggrandizing her allies Pergamum and Rhodes;[1] but her destruction of the Seleucid army immediately undid Antiochus' life-work: Sophene,[2] Armenia, Atropatene and Parthia repudiated his suzerainty and new kingdoms rose up in Elymais (Elam) and Persia. When, under Mithradates I (170–138), the Parthians succeeded in imposing their overlordship on Elymais and Persia, in conquering Media and in defeating the Bactrians, they became more powerful than their late masters, now reduced to Palestine, Syria, Mesopotamia and Cilicia.

In 171–168 the Romans had a second brush with Macedon; the monarchy was abolished and the country divided into four. Twenty years later a final flare-up provoked its annexation (148). Shortly after, a squabble in Greece proper ended the Romans' patience with Greek factionalism and in 146 the peninsula was brought under direct Roman rule. The same year wrote the final chapter of a more bitter story. Confident in Roman support the Numidians had been nibbling at the Carthaginian remnant; in 151 there were pitched battles between them and the Carthaginians. Rome seized a legalistic pretext (Carthage had agreed not to go to war without Rome's permission) to destroy the hated city, whose territory became a Roman province. The Dalmatian coast had been pacified a little previous to this (167–157).

In 170 a group of nomadic Iranian tribes dwelling on the borders of China was crushingly defeated by the Huns: these Iranians are known only through Chinese historians who called them the Yue-chi. To escape the Huns the Yue-chi moved west in a 1,000 mile, two-pronged migration that brings them into the area covered by the base-map; the Tarim basin was occupied by the smaller force, the Ili basin by the larger. Their arrival disturbed the balance existing among the Saka peoples; for a generation the tribes held to their accustomed pastures under Yue-chi suzerainty; but there were ominous rumbles.

In India, feeble inheritors of Maurya provinces lost first the Kabul valley and then the upper reaches of the Indus to the Bactrian Greeks; the new conquests became a separate kingdom under Menander who protected the Buddhists from the tide of Hindu reaction, now running strongly elsewhere in India. Also to be noted: the minor state of Paphlagonia, organized by the Bithynians in 179 to buffer their frontier with Pontus, the most virile of the Anatolian kingdoms; the re-establishment of Egypt's southern frontier at the second cataract (165).

And, now that they have extended across the whole of the Russian steppe, the Sarmatian peoples can be divided into three: the Iazygians west of the lower Dneiper; the Roxolani between the Dneiper and Don; and the stay-at-homes to the East whom we can tentatively call Alans, as this is where the Alans are believed to have come from when, in the first century A.D., they appear in the Caucasus.

---

1. The Roman Senate could be irritable as well as generous; twenty-five years later the grant to Rhodes (of Lycia and inland Caria) was revoked following a tactless display of independence by a Rhodian embassy, and, not content with this, the Senators went on to declare Delos a tax-free port, purely to divert trade away from Rhodes.

2. The western fifth of Armenia, also known as Lesser Armenia. The term Lesser Armenia was later used to denote the Pontic province nearest the upper Euphrates, Armenia proper, east of the Euphrates, being called Greater Armenia.

FINNS

TEUTONS

Balts

Slavs

La Tene CELTS

Roxolani

Iazygians

Bosporan K.

Paphlagonia

Bithynia

Pontus

Pergamum

Armenia

Atropatene

Sophene

Cappadocia

Seleucid K.

Rhodes

Ptolemaic K.

Nabataeans

ROME

Mauretania

Numidia

K. of Meroe

Alans

Sakas

Bactria

Yue-Chi
Greater & Lesser

K. of
Menander

PARTHIAN
EMPIRE

Elymais

Persia

Hadramaut

Sheba

Qataban

145 B.C.

Interwoven with the sorry political tale of division and decline following Alexander's death, is a real success story: the economic and cultural triumph of Hellenism. Ionia was rejuvenated while the welding of Egypt and Syria onto the Greek world created an economic unit of far greater size and resilience than any that existed before. The metropoli of the new unit correspondingly overshadowed their predecessors, reaching the population range 90–150,000. This order of magnitude (for which a symbol is now introduced) was first attained by Alexandria – the ostentatiously regal, unremittingly commercial paradigm of the Hellenistic capital city. Alexandria grew rapidly because within its perimeter was concentrated all the Hellenising energy of the Ptolemies. With the exception of Ptolemais – a necessity for the administration of Upper Egypt – no other Greek cities were founded in the Nile valley, which the dynasty regarded as a private estate to be farmed and taxed as meticulously as possible. The acquiescence of the fellah in a life of rural drudgery was the régime's greatest asset, as the royal bureaucracy that controlled and exploited his every activity was its most original creation; the Ptolemies had no intention of allowing either to be disturbed by city folk or city-bred ideas. Whereas in Alexandria they subsidized a university that became synonymous with Greek learning, upcountry the only buildings raised were temples dedicated to the simple-minded gods of the past.

Seleucid practice was the opposite of Ptolemaic. Both for administrative reasons – their empire was as flaccid as the Ptolemies' was tight – and to provide ethnic support for Greek rule, new cities were founded as fast as Greek immigrants could be persuaded to settle in them. The Hellenisation of the natives was always encouraged and sometimes, as in the case of the Jews, insisted upon. East of the Zagros the effort was in vain; in

Mesopotamia only superficially successful; but Syria became the seat of a genuine Hellenistic culture, and the triad of Antioch, Laodicea and Apamea, the pride and support of the dynasty. Of course these foundations lacked the autonomy which the Greeks considered to be the hallmark of the true city; the Macedonians, a people without cities, had scant sympathy for the concept and, outside the Aegean cockpit where competing monarchs posed as the champions of city rights, they ruled autocratically. In Ionia the limited freedoms restored by Alexander were little respected by his successors and though, in economic and urban terms, the Ionian revival was genuine enough, its pacemakers – Nicaea, Pergamum, Ephesus and Smyrna – were Macedonian creations devoid of the traditional city-state outlook. It was the kings and not the people of Pergamum who eventually came to dominate western Anatolia. This eclipse of classical political theory was matched by a decline in Greece proper that was absolute, not merely relative. Macedon, its gold deposits exhausted and its manpower weakened by wars and emigration, could barely hold its place among the great powers; elsewhere in the peninsula depopulation was even more rapid.

In trade, increase in volume was the achievement of the Hellenistic era; the commodities of Mediterranean traffic remained as before and, though the manufactures available showed more variety, there were no significant innovations. Nor, in spite of Alexander, were the geographical horizons of the Greeks much enlarged. The Ptolemies' interest in Red Sea adventures was stimulated by their desire to obtain from Eritrea the elephants that were essential for the self-respect of a Hellenistic general,[1] but this was a route that had been travelled by Egyptians since the days of the eighteenth dynasty. They never contacted India whose goods continued as before to be shipped to the Persian Gulf and then transported across the north of Arabia. Arabian traffic was now the monopoly of the Nabataean

Arabs whose train of caravan stations was completed on the Seleucid collapse by the acquisition of Damascus; their commercial activities were complemented by an agriculture using water-conservation techniques whose elegance has only recently been appreciated.

The Ancients had no doubt as to the reason for the rise of Rome; at times of crisis the Senate and people acted with a courage and discipline that both deserved and ensured victory. But history is crowded with unsuccessfully valorous peoples and now we seek explanations in more prosaic terms: geographical, economic or demographic. The strength of a united Italy is obvious from the number of legions fielded in the Punic wars and the course from the third century on is comprehensible. The intriguing phase is the fourth century that made Rome mistress of the peninsula. The city had no natural resources, no manufactures, no trade; in sum, no commercial justification for growing beyond the 10,000 mark. Yet grow it did and the beginnings of this growth seem to have preceded the conquests that in economic terms provide a justification for size, just as in the later period the city's expansion continually outpaced the Empire's. The need for cheap corn in ever-increasing quantities can be accepted as an important factor in Rome's overseas aggressions. First Sicily and Sardinia, then Carthaginian Africa and finally Egypt; a bigger granary was needed with each century.[2] Perhaps

(continued on page 92)

1. The Greeks first encountered war elephants during Alexander's campaign in India. Seleucus obtained 500 in return for his cession of the Indus valley and they played a crucial role at Ipsus. A contingent he took on his ill-fated expedition to Europe eventually ended up with Pyrrhus in Italy. Hannibal's were the native North African breed which did not become extinct until the second century A.D. However, after their ignominious failure at Zama elephants were little used by the military; the third century B.C. really saw the beginning and end of the fashion.

2. It has been calculated that Sicily was able to export three million bushels, Africa ten million and Egypt twenty million.

GOLD

FURS

TIN

AMBER

TIN

GOLD

WHEAT

IRON

COPPER
SILVER TIN

TIMBER

FISH

Byzantium

WINE
OIL

Nicaea

Edessa
Aleppo

Merv

Balkh

IVORY
SPICES

Hecatompylus (Damghan)

Rayy

Ecbatana (Hamadan)

POTTERY
Capua
Rome      METALWORK
Puteoli  WINE
Naples   OIL
         WOOL

Pergamum
Smyrna  Sardes
        Ephesus
        Rhodes
Delos

TIMBER

Athens

Laodicea
COPPER
Sidon
Tyre
GLASS
TEXTILES

Antioch

Apamea
Damascus

Babylon

Seleucia
Erech
Charax

COPPER

Istakhr

GOLD COPPER
MERCURY
SILVER TIN

WHEAT
Utica

Syracuse

Alexandria

Tanis

Petra

WHEAT

Cyrene

Memphis
PAPYRUS
LINEN
WHEAT
Ptolemais

GOLD

IVORY
RESINS

RESINS

GOLD
IVORY

145 B.C.

Between 140 and 135, the Yue-Chi overran Trans-oxiana. They extinguished the Greek kingdom of Bactria and set in motion a horde of Sakas which terrorized the eastern provinces of Iran until the nineties, when the Parthians regained control. Some Sakas remained as Parthian subjects[1] but King Maues led part of the horde across the Sulaiman range into India. The descent of Maues split the Greeks of the Indus valley into two small fragments, one on the left bank of the Indus, the other in the Kabul valley.

In 141 the Parthians had taken Mesopotamia from the Seleucids, but first the Sakas and then dynastic trouble prevented them from profiting by the final Seleucid collapse. The easy pickings went instead to the Armenian king Tigranes who, after repudiating the Parthian overlordship imposed on him at his accession, relieved his late masters of Atropatene and northern Mesopotamia and then moved on to seize Cilicia and most of Syria (83). The broom was wielded too rapidly to sweep clean: in 74 the cities of Seleucia-in-Syria and Acre still harboured Seleucid princes and several inland towns were in the hands of the Ituraean and Nabataean Arabs. To the south, a renascent and belligerent Jewish state had been autonomous since 129. The Jews had recuperated under the tolerant rule of the Persians and their furious rejection of Hellenism had fortunately for them been delayed until the Seleucids were safely in decline. In the long run the success of the Maccabees in what seemed at the time a hopeless cause was to be an unfortunate precedent.

The obvious supremacy of Rome in the Mediterranean world and the inevitability of her further advance led the last king of Pergamum to will his state to Rome (133); western Cilicia was annexed as the rest of an anti-piracy campaign (102); Ptolemaic Egypt and the states of central Anatolia became officially Roman-protected.[2] These acqui-sitions added new burdens to the over-strained Senatorial government, which displayed its growing inability to cope with its business in a brush-fire war with King Jugurtha of Numidia (110–105). Roman honour was only saved by a general of comparatively obscure birth, Marius, who immediately became the mascot of the Popular opposition at home. With Jugurtha disposed of, the Senate enlarged Mauretania at Numidia's expense; Marius was rushed home to deal with a new threat – the impending invasion of the Cimbri and Teutones. These two Celtic tribes of the middle Danube had been on the move since about 115; in 113 they had made a tentative stab at the north of Italy and defeated a Roman army, but then turned away and passed north of the Alps to Gaul. Except in the north-east, where they were repulsed by the Belgae, the strongest of the Gallic confederations, they were everywhere successful and the Roman part of Gaul was pillaged along with the rest. Easy victories gave them such a contempt for Roman arms that in 102 they decided to make a two-pronged attack on Italy. Marius annihilated the horde that attempted the coastal route, and, though in doing so he had to allow the other an unopposed entry to the Po valley via the Alps, he caught and destroyed this group the following year.[3]

Alarmed at Marius' enhanced popularity, the Senate determined to make the least possible use of his services thereafter. They refused him command of the eastern provinces where punishment was overdue for Mithradates VI of Pontus (during the decade 110–100, Mithradates had annexed the Bosporan kingdom, the Crimea, and the Roman-protected states of Galatia and Cappadocia) and he was allowed only a minor part in the Social War of 91–88 in which the Italian provincials, provoked by the Romans' refusal to allow them full citizenship, rose in rebellion. The repression of the Italians proved not too difficult once the extension of the franchise had been promised, and produced a successful Senatorial general in Sulla.

To him the Senate gave the coveted command in the East. Before he left, Sulla used his legions to consolidate the aristocratic position at home, Marius only avoiding execution by fleeing to Africa. Meanwhile Mithradates had seized the opportunity offered by the Social War to overrun all Anatolia and even invade Greece. Sulla had little difficulty in driving him back into his own territory and forcing him to sue for peace, but the terms dictated – Mithradates kept his kingdom – were scarcely harsh; for while Sulla had been engaged in the campaign, Marius had returned to Rome, overthrown the Senate and instituted a Popular dictatorship. Sulla hurried home to find Marius dead of a stroke; his veterans made short work of the Popular levies and the restoration of Senatorial rule that followed was even bloodier than its previous overthrow.

About 115 control of the Kingdom of Saba in the Yemen passed into the hands of the Himyarite Arabs; the new dynasty gradually extended its control over the whole of Arabia Felix, absorbing Qataban in 50 and the Hadramaut in A.D. 100.

1. Particularly in the province henceforth known as Seistan (Sakastan). This became first the fief and later, c.80, the quasi-independent kingdom of the Surens (Pahlavas, Indo-Parthians), a Parthian family which had played a prominent part in the re-conquest.

The Arab kingdom of Charax which arose just inside Parthian territory in 128 was reduced to vassalage within a few years of its foundation.

2. With the exception of the two fragments in India, all the Greek states were now under Roman rule or control and on this and succeeding maps the Roman boundary is given the thickness previously used to mark the perimeter of the Greek world.

3. Though they have given their name to the German linguistic group, the Teutones were *not* Teutons. The Romans used the term German geographically and when they said that the Teutones, Belgae or Bastarnae were Germans they meant only that these Celtic peoples had originally lived in Germany (that is, east of the Rhine and north of the upper Danube).

TEUTONS

Goths

Belgae

Lesser
Yue-Chi

Greater
Yue-Chi

Greek Principalities

Saka K.

ⓒ

Suren
Kingdom

K. of Pontus

PARTHIAN
EMPIRE

R O M E

Paphlagonia
Galatia
Cappadocia

Armenian
Empire

Elymais

Persis

Charax

Seleucia
Ituraeans
Acre
Jews

Mauretania

Numidia

Nabataeans

Ptolemaic K.

Hadramaut

Himyarite
K.

Qataban

K. of Meroe

ⓒ Cimbri and Teutones

74 B.C.

Sulla's position as the Senatorial champion was inherited by his lieutenant, Pompey, who put an end to the Populist remnants in Spain (76–71), cleared the Mediterranean of pirates (67) and in 66 took command in the East where, once again, hostilities had broken out with Mithradates. This time Mithradates had as his ally Tigranes of Armenia; but Tigranes' jerry-built empire did not survive its first major test. Pompey's victories were quick and conclusive: he followed them up by making the direct settlement of eastern affairs that the Senate had been avoiding for the last century (64). The coastline from Pontus to Egypt was annexed and the kingdoms of the interior given definitive status as Roman vassals. In Anatolia there were two major client states, the kingdoms of Cappadocia and Galatia (this last the reward of a chieftain who had loyally assisted the Romans during the Mithradatic wars) plus minor principalities in Paphlagonia, Lycaonia and Cilicia. Beyond, Armenia and the Caucasian principalities of Colchis and Iberia were required to recognize Roman suzerainty which extended, somewhat less certainly, over the Iranian Albani. To the south, Syria was made a province, Emesa, the Ituraeans, Jews and Nabataeans, client-states.

Pompey's progress alarmed the Senate, which was now beginning to feel strong enough to dispense with a protector. The Senators waited until the conqueror had dismissed his soldiers and then rebuffed the very reasonable demands he made on their behalf. Inevitably Pompey turned to the enemies of the Senatorial oligarchy; Caesar, who controlled the remnant of the Marian Popular party, and Crassus, the archetypal plutocrat, all too eager to buy himself into history. The Senate found itself pushed to one side by this triumvirate and thereafter Pompey ruled in Rome while Caesar and Crassus took up the military commands they coveted. Both hoped to gain victories that would give them the same stature as Pompey and both indulged in gratuitous aggression to satisfy this ambition. In a remorseless series of campaigns between 58 and 51 Caesar conquered Gaul, defeated an invasion of Germans from across the Rhine, invested his whole enterprise with romance by reconnoitering the hitherto fabulous island of Britain, and won the devotion of an army that had become the most formidable in the Roman world. Crassus also made his mark. Leading the legions of the East against Parthia, he was barely across the frontier when his force was cut off and shot to pieces by the Saka bowmen of the Parthians' Suren ally. Crassus perished in the débâcle (at Carrhae, 53). It seemed as if Pompey's eastern settlement would be overthrown by the victors; but as Parthian quarrelled with Suren and Caesar with Pompey, the war petered out. Only Armenia and the Transcaucasian peoples passed out of Roman control.

Caesar's mounting reputation cast a shadow over Pompey's achievements and the resulting coolness between the two was quickly exploited by the Senate. Reminding Pompey that he was Sulla's heir and that it was his duty to protect the constitution, the Senators persuaded him to break with Caesar. They were confident that he could handle the upstart and that they could handle him. But Caesar moved too fast for the new allies, seizing Rome by a forced march (50) and Spain in a six-week campaign (49). At Pharsalus, in 48, the tenacity of his legions gave him a complete victory over the army Pompey had gathered in Greece and from there he went on to make a clean sweep of the East (47). Africa (46) and Spain, which had revolted again (45). The man who had gone into politics to pay his debts returned to Rome with the Empire in his pocket and Cleopatra, the last of the Ptolemies, on his arm. Caesar's political administration was like his generalship, active and efficient, but behind the urgency of the reformer lay the restlessness of an opportunist. In the middle of preparations for invasions of Parthia and Dacia – both unnecessary as Parthia was quiet and the Dacian kingdom collapsed of its own accord within a few years – he was assassinated by a diehard aristocratic clique (44).

For information about the eastern third of the map we have to rely on Chinese historians whose chronological framework is not always easy to relate to our own. About the middle of the last century B.C. the Surens invaded the Indus valley, broke the power of the Sakas and deposed the last Indo-Greek princes. The Yue-Chi seem to have remained fairly quiet. The main Chinese interest in the region lay to the north whither a part of the Hunnish nation had fled (44) after a catastrophic defeat by the forces of the Emperor Wu Ti of China. These western Huns recuperated rapidly in their new home, soon reducing to vassalage the Iranian tribes of the Ili basin. The Chinese decided, somewhat ambitiously, to break up the new Hunnish power before it had time to consolidate. In 36 an expeditionary force succeeded in doing just that, an event that marks the apogee of the Early Han dynasty's military prowess and still stands as one of the most remarkable achievements of Chinese arms.

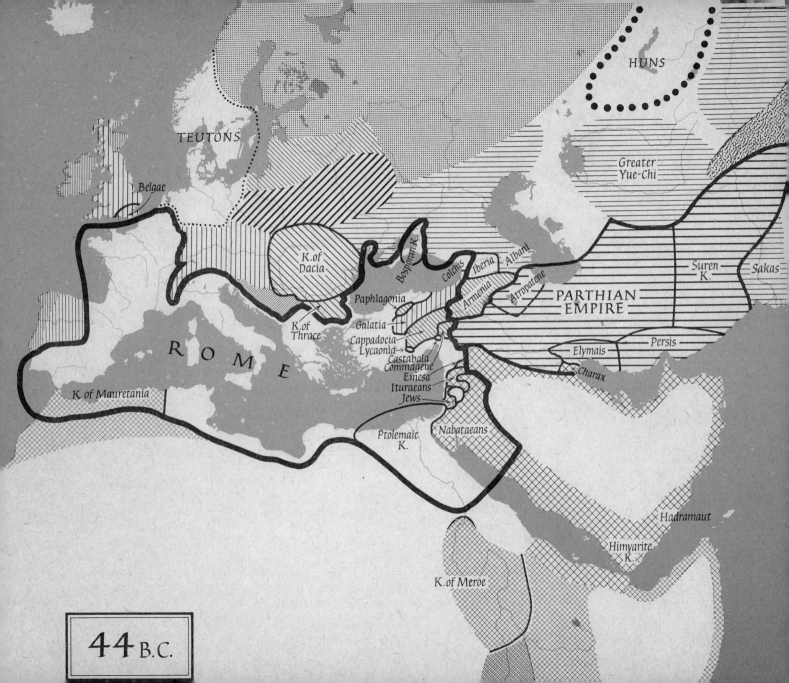

TEUTONS

HUNS

Greater
Yue-Chi

Belgae

K. of
Dacia

Bosporan K.

Colchis

Iberia

Albani

PARTHIAN
EMPIRE

Suren
K.

Sakas

Paphlagonia

Armenia

Atropatene

K. of
Thrace

Galatia

ROME

Cappadocia
Lycaonia

Castabala
Commagene
Emesa
Ituraeans
Jews

Elymais

Persis

Charax

K. of Mauretania

Ptolemaic
K.

Nabataeans

Hadramaut

Himyarite
K.

K. of Meroe

**44** B.C.

Though Caesar's assassination was the signal for political reaction, Republicanism was no longer a vital force. Once Caesar's heir, Octavius, and Caesar's lieutenant, Anthony, had come to terms with one another, it took only the single battle of Phillipi (42) to make an end of the Republican party. The Empire was divided between the victors: Anthony, the most experienced general, taking the East and the Parthian problem, and Octavius the West; while Africa was given to Lepidus, a myopic grandee whom Anthony and Octavius had been carrying around with them to reassure the conservatives.

Anthony wrested the suzerainty of Transcaucasia, Armenia and Atropatene from the Parthians but casualties were heavy and the replacements promised by Octavius never seemed to arrive. He consoled himself with Cleopatra; in re-creating the Empire of the Ptolemies for her he alienated his depleted legions and when the inevitable break with Octavius came they promptly deserted him (Actium, 31). Anthony committed suicide, as did Cleopatra after her capture; her son by Caesar was tidied away into a small box.

With unchallengeable hegemony, and the new name of Augustus (27), Octavius now gave the Mediterranean world what it had lacked for so long, internal peace and sensible frontiers. Neglected enclaves in Spain and the Alps were soon pacified: the major advance was in central and eastern Europe where his generals gradually pushed forward to reach the Danube along its full length. This simplification of the frontier (begun before the war with Anthony but not completed till 12) suggested a further improvement, the annexation of Germany up to the Elbe. The northern half of this area was occupied between 12 and A.D. 5 but on the eve of the final move (against the Marcomanni, the only politically organised Teutonic tribe) the new Danubian

76

provinces flared into revolt. Though they were soon brought to heel, Augustus, feeling that his gains required further digestion, called off the offensive against the Marcomanni, and when the three-legion garrison of the north German province was annihilated in an ambush (A.D. 9) he gave up the whole idea. Rhine[1] and Danube were to mark the limits of the Empire in Europe.

Potentially the most embarrassing part of Augustus' Caesarian inheritance was his adoptive father's declared intention of marching against the Parthians. Augustus saw that the Parthian empire had no power to sustain an offensive: when he had restored Rome's strategic and moral position by re-asserting suzerainty over Armenia and Transcaucasia (20) and obtaining the return of the standards lost at Carrhae, he was able to ignore chauvinistic pressure for a radical solution of the Parthian problem. His main concern in the East was the Romanization of the areas already within the Empire. Fiefs that had been the reward of loyalty in more troubled times were annexed as they became paying propositions: in Anatolia, Galatia was absorbed in 25, Paphlagonia in 6; Pontus (re-established as a kingdom by Anthony), Cappadocia and Commagene alone outlasted Augustus' reign. Palestine, the whole of which was ruled by Herod the Great from 37 to 4, was divided on his death and the largest and most important of the three resulting tetrarchies[2] became the province of Judea nine years later. (John the Baptist was beheaded by one of the surviving tetrarchs; Christ crucified by order of the Governor of Judea.)

Before Augustus the Romans had raised armies only for specific tasks, disbanding them when these were accomplished. Augustus created a standing army of twenty-five legions; their positions at his death are marked on this map. The equivalent of a twenty-sixth legion, the Praetorian Guard, garrisoned Italy and protected the Emperor's person. Each legion consisted of about 5,000 men (ten cohorts of 480 men each). In

addition to the 130,000 legionaries and guards (recruited from Roman citizens) there was an approximately equal number of auxiliary troops (provincials or even barbarians). The distribution of the cohort-sized auxiliary units roughly follows that of the legions.

Augustus' power originally rested, as completely as had Caesar's, on the loyalty of the legionary, but throughout his reign he worked to reconcile the Republicans and encourage their participation (in roles chosen by him) in the new order. He restored a pretence of constitutionalism by accumulating traditional offices until these were sufficient to explain and legitimize his preeminent position; he returned the government of the pacified provinces to the Senate while retaining under his personal control the more 'difficult' ones (which contained the legions) and Egypt[3] (whose corn made up the greater part of the dole of the Roman plebs). Caesar's dazzling talents had kept the Mediterranean world in turmoil: the grey genius of Augustus created peace and prosperity, and the machinery for its continuance. He used men well, shunned the spectacular, and died in bed.

1. The North Sea coast was retained up to the Elbe till A.D. 17, when the protectorate was reduced to the area of modern Holland. Under Claudius the frontier was finally withdrawn to the line of the Rhine.
2. Strictly a quarter of a kingdom but frequently used in a sense equivalent to principality.
3. Annexed on the defeat of Anthony. On the Red Sea coast to the south of Egypt note the appearance of the kingdom of Abyssinia, the first political expression of the long-standing Arabic colonization of the Eritrean coast. During this preliminary phase in its history it is often referred to as the kingdom of Axum, after its capital town.

FINNS

HUNS

TEUTONS

Burgundians

Gepids

Belgae

Balts

Goths

Slavs

Sennones

Roxolani

Alans

Greater
Yue-Chi

Hermanduri

Iazygians

Bosporan K.

Marcomanni

Quadi

Iberia

Suren
K.

Pontus

Armenia

Atropatene

PARTHIAN
EMPIRE

Commagene

Adiabene

Thracian Principalities

ROMAN EMPIRE

Cappadocia

Elymais

Persis

Castabala

Charax

Emesa

Ituraeans

K. of Mauretania

Herodian
Principalities

Nabataeans

Hadramaut

Himyarite
K.

K. of
Abyssinia

K. of Meroe

■ Roman Legion

A.D. 14

The governmental machine created by Augustus continued to function smoothly during the reign of his astringent step-son, Tiberius (14–37), and even the antics of Gaius Caligula (37–41) who dismissed the whole system as so much claptrap surrounding an autocratic power that he, in contrast, nakedly paraded, did little to disturb the Empire outside of Rome. On Caligula's assassination, the Praetorians selected his uncle, the elderly Claudius; the Senate's acquiescence in this choice marks the absorption of the Republican tradition by the Imperial.

Claudius (41–54) showed unexpected initiative. The pacification of Spain and Dalmatia had proceeded to the point where a legion could be withdrawn from each; two further legions were raised. Four legions would, it was (correctly) calculated, suffice for the conquest of Britain, a safe project sanctified by the memory of the deified Julius. The southern third of the country was rapidly overrun (43–47); the halt called at this stage was prolonged throughout the reign of Claudius' step-son Nero by the revolt of Boadicea (61).

Nero had troubles, particularly in the East. First there was a ten-year war with Parthia over Armenia,[1] then in 66 the Jews, who had never reconciled themselves to Roman rule, rose in bitter revolt. The setbacks in Britain and Palestine are often quoted as reasons for Nero's loss of popularity, as are a fire and near-famine in Rome itself, but it is difficult to believe that his reign would have been longer if it had been more fortunate. His position required of him little more than the appearance of gravity, yet this was a role that Nero, the self-declared actor, was never able to sustain. When the Romans had only just accustomed themselves to the sight of a palace in Rome, Nero cleared a quarter of the city to create the setting for a country house. The ease of the pastoral life was delightfully heightened by the thought of the sweaty bustle outside, but few Romans appreciated the conceit. The end came in 67, when the governor of Spain proclaimed the Emperor's unworthiness and marched on Rome. Beside the Praetorians, Nero had a newly raised legion in Italy (making the total for this map twenty-eight); he was unable to interest either in his survival and the last of the Julio-Claudians died by his own shaky hand. The usurper was soon replaced by the Praetorians' candidate; he, in his turn, by the commander of the Rhine legions, but the final say was with the legions of the East. In 69, they fought their way into Rome on behalf of Vespasian, the general in charge of the suppression of the Jewish revolt.

Throughout the period the absorption of the client-kingdoms continued. Cappadocia was annexed by Tiberius, Mauretania by Caligula, Thrace by Claudius and Pontus by Nero. The Ituraean principalities were divided between the province of Syria and the surviving Herodian tetrarchy, that of Agrippa II. Commagene, though annexed by Tiberius, was restored and enlarged (by the addition of part of Cilicia) by Caligula.

In the early part of the first century the clan of Kushan established a paramountcy among the Yue-Chi tribes and initiated a new expansionist phase in their history. The major drive was into India where the Suren Kingdom was conquered (50–75), but the appearance in the Caucasus of a new Sarmatian people, the Alans, may be a reflection of Kushan pressure westward. The Alan movement caused secondary westward shifts among the inhabitants of the steppe, the Iazygians, as end-men, being pushed off to the Theiss plain. This rearrangement was complete in Claudius' time.

1. This ended in compromise (63), a scion of the Parthian royal house being recognized as King of Armenia, but under Roman suzerainty. The two-legion reinforcement of the eastern army that the war necessitated was obtained by reducing the garrisons of Spain and Dalmatia by a further legion apiece. These legions remained in the East thereafter.

TEUTONS

Burgundians

Gepids

Geoths

Sennones

Quadi

Hermanduri

Marcomanni

Iazygians

Dacians

Roxolani

Bosporan K.

Colchis

Iberia

Alans

HUNS

KUSHANS

Atropatene

Hyrcania

PARTHIAN EMPIRE

ROMAN EMPIRE

Armenia

Adiabene

Elymais

Persis

Charax

Sophene

Lesser Armenia

Edessa

Commagene-Cilicia

Emesa

K. of Agrippa II

Jewish revolt

Nabataeans

K. of Meroe

K. of Abyssinia

Himyarite K.

Hadramaut

■ Roman Legion

A.D. 67

The Flavian dynasty founded by Vespasian (69–79) gave the Empire professional government once more. Emesa, Commagene, and Armenia Minor were annexed, the Rhine–Danube angle rounded off and the occupation of Britain carried up to the Highlands. Titus (79–81), Vespasian's elder son and the conqueror of Jerusalem, did not long survive his father; Domitian, the younger (81–96), left no heir. The Senate appointed the aged Nerva to the vacant throne and he placated the restive soldiery by naming the seasoned general Trajan as his successor.[1]

Domitian's reign had seen hard fighting on the Danube, particularly against the Dacians. Trajan (98–117) massed ten legions for a war that finally broke the Dacian power and made of their territory Rome's only trans-Danubian province. Then he turned east. Agrippa II's little kingdom had already been absorbed and Nabataea reduced to provincial status (106); now Armenia was made a province (114) and Parthia invaded (115). With Adiabene and Mesopotamia conquered in a single campaign, the Emperor stood in Charax, thinking aloud of Alexander. But he was sixty-three and the next year he died. Hadrian (117–38), his nephew and successor, immediately pulled back to the Euphrates, Armenia reverted to the role of client kingdom and only the suzerainty of Edessa remained as a souvenir of the greatest of the soldier-emperors. The wall in Britain, with its corollary, the abandonment of southern Scotland, was one of many works proclaiming the re-stabilization of the frontier.

Between the end of Nero's reign and the end of Hadrian's, six legions were raised (three in the turmoil of Nero's overthrow, one by Domitian and two by Trajan) and six lost (two in a revolt by the Rhine auxiliaries during the wars of Nero's successors, two in Domitian's Dacian wars, one in a British war and one in the final messianic Jewish revolt of Simon-bar-Kochba–these last, events of Hadrian's reign). But if the total of twenty-eight is the same as before the distribution shows an eastward shift in the military centre of gravity. The defence of Anatolia required the transfer of two legions and the Danube frontier an additional four; these troops were obtained by running down the garrisons of the Rhine (by three), Britain and Egypt (by one each), and by deploying the legion that had been in Italy in Nero's last days. To minimize the consequences of military revolt, legions were now stationed in isolation: the last of the double camps favoured by Augustus was broken up by Hadrian.

The Chinese had decided that a forward policy was the answer to their perennial nomad problem and in the last quarter of the first century they established control over the Tarim basin. Frequent revolts and the immense distances involved finally discouraged them; the protectorate was allowed to lapse in 106. In fact it may have been rendered untenable by the Kushans, who shortly after this occupied at least the western half of the Tarim area. This happened in the reign of Kanishka, a convert to Buddhism and the greatest of the Kushan sovereigns. His dates are uncertain but fall within the period 120–60.

1. The first Emperor to have been born outside Italy, Trajan came from a Roman colonial family resident in Spain.

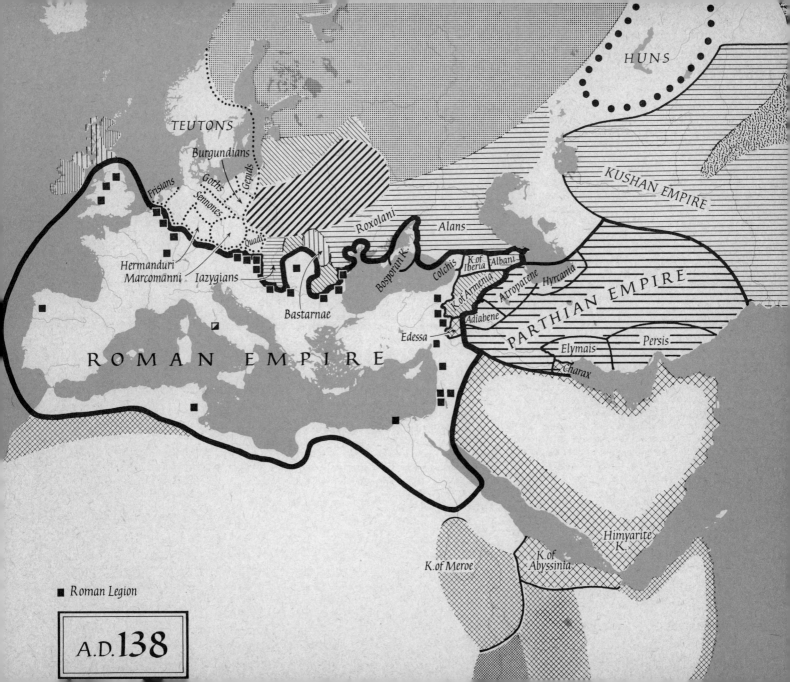

HUNS

TEUTONS

Burgundians

Goths

Gepids

Frisians

Semnones

Quadi

Hermanduri

Marcomanni

Iazygians

Bastarnae

Roxolani

Alans

KUSHAN EMPIRE

Bosporan K.

Colchis

K. of Iberia

Albani

K. of Armenia

Atropatene

Hyrcania

Adiabene

PARTHIAN EMPIRE

Edessa

Elymais

Persis

Charax

ROMAN EMPIRE

Himyarite K.

K. of Meroe

K. of Abyssinia

■ Roman Legion

A.D. 138

A.D. 230

The defensive policy to which Hadrian returned continued in operation throughout the second century A.D., a period generally considered the golden age of the Roman Empire and certainly one during which the military effort required for the security of the Mediterranean world was at a minimum. The succession passed smoothly from Hadrian to Antoninus Pius to Marcus Aurelius, each chosen by his predecessor for proven efficiency and probity. Marcus (161–80) spoilt the sequence by bequeathing the purple to his foolish son Commodus, whose assassination provoked a civil war similar to that at Nero's death. The British, Danubian and eastern armies each proclaimed their candidates; not surprisingly it was the choice of the biggest battalions, the Danubian commander Septimius Severus, who made good. He ruled from 193 to 211; the Empire then passed through an increasingly alarming series of his relatives, the last of whom was assassinated in 235.

The maintenance of the Hadrianic frontier (modified only by the conquest of southern Scotland[1] in 142) was apparently a matter of little difficulty, but already the Empire's margin of superiority was being eroded by the rising numbers of the barbarians. As a result of overcrowding in the Vistula region, the eastern Germans started to move south. This movement, which was probably more of a steady dribble than a fifth century-style *Volkwanderung*, resulted in the formation of the Gothic nation of southern Russia in the second half of the second century and of the Gepid nation in the Carpathians in the first half of the next, while the Asding branch of the Vandals replaced the Iazygians as the dominant element in the Theiss plain. Just as ominously for the Romans, the many small tribes of the Rhine frontier were entering into permanent federations – the super-tribes of Alemanni and Frank.

82

Another threat to the security of the Empire came with the overthrow of the Parthian monarchy by the Persian Ardashir (226). The Sassanid dynasty he founded created a much more tightly knit nation than the Parthian and strove to revive the imperial Iranian spirit by constantly harking back to the glories and frontiers of the Achaemenids. During the decline of the Parthians the Romans had made considerable advances in northern Mesopotamia (in 161–5 and more particularly under Septimius Severus in 194–9) so the Sassanids had a ready-made and entirely legal grievance. But strategically their position was unfavourable, for the Armenian kings, being of Parthian blood, naturally allied themselves with the Romans against the usurpers: perhaps because of this the first Sassanid attempt on Roman Mesopotamia failed to win any ground at all. The dynasty did better in the East, where, at about the date of this map, the Kushan Empire split into several principalities. The Sassanids appear to have rapidly established an ascendancy over the nearest of these, but their claim to have made the Oxus and Indus their frontiers seems over-stated, reflecting influence, not authority. The Kushan states certainly continued in existence as political entities until the fifth century.

By 230 the legionary total had risen to thirty-three. Marcus had raised two for his war against the Marcomanni and they remained on the upper Danube at its end. Septimius Severus raised three for his Parthian war and left two in the new province of (northern) Mesopotamia. The third he kept near Rome as a reminder to the Praetorians to behave.

1. The Roman frontier in Europe, as it does more obviously in Africa and the East, by and large corresponds with the limit of intensive agriculture. Economically the rational frontier in Britain was about half way up and Hadrian's wall was a fair military translation of this, but there was always a feeling that, after all, the place was an island, and if you could get to the end you wouldn't need a frontier at all. Accordingly, the annexation of Scotland was attempted at intervals but always failed because the legions could not supply themselves in such sparsely populated country.

FINNS

HUNS

TEUTONS

Irish

Picts

Jutes
Angles
Frisians

Balts

Kushan Principalities

Saxons
Lombards
Burgundians

Slays

Alemanni

Franks

Quadi

Gepids

Goths

Roxolani

Alans

Marcomanni

Siling
Vandals

Asding Vandals

Bosporan K.

Colchis

K. of
Iberia

K. of Armenia

PERSIAN EMPIRE

ROMAN EMPIRE

Himyarite
K.

K. of Meroe

K. of
Abyssinia

■ Roman Legion

A.D. 230

Military disasters during the first two and a half centuries of the Empire's existence being few and peripheral, the Mediterranean community was able to realize its full wealth, and though it must be remembered that given the limitations of classical technology the overwhelming proportion of this wealth must have been agricultural, the increasing number of towns of minor rank and the burgeoning splendour of the three metropoli have always been considered the great socio-economic achievement of the *Pax Romana*. Rome's growth was, of course, parasitic, its income directly or indirectly tributary, but in the provinces fine towns are rightly read as testimonials to the ordered continuity of life within the Empire. A hundred cities from Spain to the Syrian Desert repeated the impressive apparatus of Roman urbanism: basilica, aqueduct, theatre, and amphitheatre. With prosperity at its peak under the Severi it would be surly to note that these were heavy appendages.

In the East the growth of the cities was fortified by the extended range of their commerce. During the first century A.D. there were two important additions to the traditional trading network: the 'silk route' stretching across Central Asia which put Antioch in tenuous contact with China, and the direct passage across the Arabian Sea by which Alexandrian merchants obtained access to India. The staple of the trans-Asian route, Chinese silk, had an instant success in the West despite its high price, the sumptuary regulations of disapproving emperors being ineffective in a society geared for conspicuous consumption. The only Mediterranean equivalent, the rough silk of Cos, was driven off the market and forgotten so completely that the nature of silk became a subject for rumour and speculation. Silk is an expensive material to start with and a slow passage through the marts and tolls of the ancient world's longest trade route inevitably multiplied its cost, but the Romans were probably right when they protested that the Parthians grossly overcharged them. There was little they could do about it for the Parthians' complete control of the last stage of the route gave them an effective monopoly *vis-à-vis* the Romans.

A similar situation with regard to the Indian trade was averted by the discovery of the monsoons blowing between the exit from the Red Sea and the west coast of India. The non-stop crossing made possible by these winds led to a greatly increased traffic. At the Egyptian end the Imperial administration built roads and ports along the eastern seaboard and refurbished the Nile–Red Sea canal. This last proved a disappointment as it had to Persians and Ptolemies, because the winds at the northern end of the Red Sea are unreliable and merchants preferred to trans-ship at the level of Thebes and take the safe passage down the Nile.

It might be expected that at a time when the Kushans controlled both Transoxiana and the Indus valley silk would be among India's exports, but in fact the quantity the Romans received from this source seems to have been too small to have had any effect on the silk route proper. The major goods supplied were ivory, ebony and spices. The term 'spice' covers a variety of organic and mineral substances traded in small amounts: condiments, resins, pigments, dyes and mordants.[1] The most important Indian spice was pepper and with its increased availability in the West its inferior rival, the silphium of Cyrenaica, followed Coan silk into oblivion. Resins have already been mentioned as the typical export of Arabia;[2] the Indian product in this category was spikenard. Resins were also produced in East Africa and, within the borders of the Empire, in the Levant. Pigments such as malachite, vermilion, azurite and ochre came principally from Spain. As for dyes the most famous was the purple (actually crimson) of Tyre, an incredibly costly material obtained by allowing a mass of shellfish to rot in the sun. Commercially the most significant was the carmine produced from insects of the *coccidae* family in Spain, Anatolia and India. The cheaper dye-stuffs – woad (indigo), saffron and madder – were little traded because the plants from which they derive are of common occurrence. The usual mordant[2] was alum which was obtained from Anatolia and, via Egypt, from the Sahara.

Arabian trade suffered from the loss of the Indian transit traffic; the Nabataeans' importance declined and the emphasis shifted north towards the boom towns of Palmyra and Hatra on the last stretch of the silk route.

The Romans were always worrying over the gold loss that they felt sure resulted from their foreign trade, but although India, where gold was scarce and by Mediterranean standards overvalued, certainly received a considerable amount of bullion, the Empire very likely earned enough by the export of its manufactures to cover the cost of its imports. The percolation of classical art motifs into Central Asia suggests a wide demand for Roman goods; their quality and variety were generally superior to the native equivalents and in glassware the cities of the Levant had no rivals.[3] In line with this, archaeological evidence strongly suggests that Rome's exports were healthy, and, as pronouncements on the gold drain often form part of moralistic ruminations on luxuries in general and tom fool foreign luxuries in particular, they should probably not be taken too seriously anyway.

1. Mordants are substances used to modify the colour of dyes and to render them fast.
2. See page 44.
3. The invention, in Egypt or Syria at the beginning of the first century, of the technique of glass-blowing brought the price of glass utensils down to the point where their use became general; at the other end of the scale were the complex millefiori and cameo pieces of the Alexandrian master craftsmen.

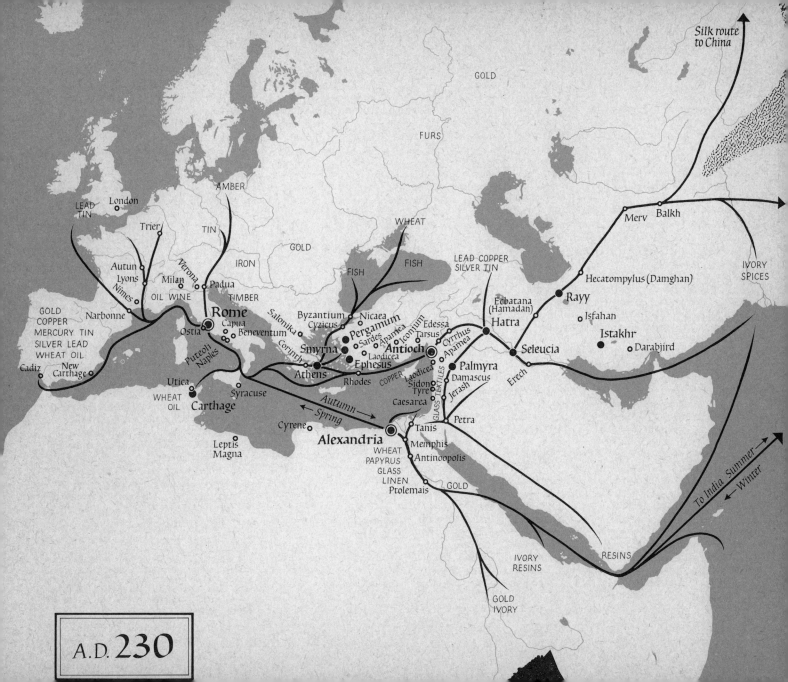

LEAD
TIN
London
Trier
AMBER
TIN
Autun
Lyons
Nimes
Milan
Verona
Padua
OIL WINE
IRON
GOLD
TIMBER
Narbonne
OIL
WINE
GOLD
COPPER
MERCURY TIN
SILVER LEAD
WHEAT OIL
Cadiz
New
Carthage
Utica
Carthage
Syracuse
WHEAT
OIL
Cyrene
Leptis
Magna
GOLD
FURS
GOLD
WHEAT
FISH
FISH
Rome
Capua
Beneventum
Salonika
Corinth
Ostia
Puteoli
Naples
Athens
Byzantium
Cyzicus
Nicaea
Pergamum
Sardes
Apamea
Smyrna
Laodicea
Ephesus
Rhodes
COPPER
Edessa
Iconium
Tarsus
Antioch
Cyrrhus
Apamea
Laodicea
Sidon
Tyre
Jerash
Caesarea
Damascus
Palmyra
Petra
GLASS TEXTILES
LEAD COPPER
SILVER TIN
Hatra
Seleucia
Erech
Ecbatana
(Hamadan)
Rayy
Hecatompylus (Damghan)
Isfahan
Istakhr
Darabjird
Merv
Balkh
Silk route
to China
IVORY
SPICES
Alexandria
Tanis
Memphis
Antinoopolis
Ptolemais
WHEAT
PAPYRUS
GLASS
LINEN
GOLD
Autumn
Spring
IVORY
RESINS
GOLD
IVORY
RESINS
To India Summer
Winter

A.D. 230

The command of a Roman army went with the governorship of the province it garrisoned. Aristocratic birth and satisfactory performance in a defined series of military and civil positions being necessary qualifications for this top job, the Senate, now the guardian of the Imperial tradition, rarely felt any inclination to argue when the army raised a governor-general to the purple; the move was illegal but the piece orthodox. Then in 235 the Rhine legions followed their murder of the final Severan by the proclamation of Maximin, a Thracian soldier of obscure birth and exclusively military experience. At this the Senators baulked. Italy was armed and Maximin's invasion held up long enough for his men to turn against him. They killed him, then they killed the Senate's candidates (238). After an uneasy pause, compromise prevailed in the emperors Decius, Gallus and Valerian, who were generals and gentlemen (244–60). Their total lack of success destroyed the prestige of the old Imperial system and with it the resistance to frank military despotism. To Valerian's son Gallienus (260–68) succeeded a series of emperors[1] who had risen from the ranks of the new model army he had created. They were all of Illyrian peasant stock, as was the core of this army.

By 250 the soldiers' indiscipline had severely weakened the central authority, while attempts to buy their loyalty had driven the exchequer into bankruptcy. However, the immediate danger to the Empire lay less in the turbulence of the legions than in their obsolescence. The inertia which had developed in the Roman military machine (Septimius Severus permitted the legionary to marry and work a small-holding) contrasted ominously with the advances in cavalry equipment and tactics that were being made by the Iranians. The storm broke in 251 when the Goths invaded the Balkans – henceforth their stamping ground –

86

and overthrew Decius, the first emperor ever to be killed by barbarians. Five years later the Rhine frontier shattered and Gaul was overrun by the Franks and Alemanni. Their bands penetrated into Spain and Italy while the Goths reached across the now exhausted Balkans into Anatolia. During the same decade the Persians conquered Armenia and one by one reduced the Mesopotamian frontier-fortresses; in 260 they captured the Emperor Valerian, broke through to Syria and put Antioch to the sack. At this nadir of Imperial fortune, Gallienus held the centre of the Empire; Britain, Gaul and Spain recognized Postumus, an emperor created by the reviving Rhine army, and the East a third, Macrianus. Gallienus disposed of the latter and deputed the East to the Sheikh of Palmyra, Odenathus, who, using local levies, drove back the Sassanids. The Gothic invasion of 268 was broken by Gallienus himself; but the Palmyrenes seceded, taking Syria with them, and unity appeared as far away as ever. Yet under Gallienus the army had recovered its efficiency and the Illyrian emperors were able to lead it to victory over rebel and barbarian alike. In particular, Aurelian (270–75), by smashing the Gallic and Palmyrene sub-empires and formally abandoning Dacia and the Rhine–Danube angle,[2] drew the outline of the restored Empire, while Diocletian (284–305) by completing and codifying thirty years of desperate military and administrative extemporization, translated arbitrary army rule into a new system of government, the Tetrarchy.

With wars liable to break out simultaneously along the whole frontier from Britain to Egypt, the precariously re-established unity of the Empire, though beautiful to behold, was a strategic disadvantage. Each front required an Emperor, as much to prevent the troops from proclaiming one of their own as to conduct operations. A year after his accession Diocletian made a co-emperor, Maximian, to whom he delegated the West; in 293 he appointed two

junior emperors ('Caesars' as opposed to 'Augusti') who undertook the more pressing military tasks. Caesar Constantius fought on the Rhine and in 296 re-conquered Britain (in revolt since 287); Caesar Galerius was employed first on the Danube and after 297 against Persia. The triumphant conclusion of the Persian war gave Rome her most favourable Mesopotamian frontier to date.

The changes in the army are so far-reaching as to require the use of new symbols. By the mid third century it had become impossible to move legions about as in the old days, for, even if the local situation permitted its withdrawal, the bulk of the legion was too firmly attached to its camp to give more than grudging service outside its own province. Instead, reinforcements for threatened frontiers were obtained by taking a double-strength cohort from every legion on a quiet sector. At the same time new-style independent cavalry units were raised. As temporary detachments became permanent the army split into two: a mobile army of cavalry and 1,000-man legions, and a garrison army tied to fortifications. Each Augustus kept part of the mobile army under his direct command; Maximian's was normally stationed in the Po valley guarding the entry to Italy, Diocletian's at Nicomedia. The remainder was split into three forces, stationed immediately behind the Rhine, Danube and Eastern frontiers at Trier, Sirmium and Antioch. In manpower the garrison army was probably equivalent to the whole pre-crisis army; the mobile army of some hundred thousand men accordingly represents the extra military burden borne by the Empire under the Tetrarchy.

1. Claudius II, Probus, Aurelian, Carus, Diocletian and Maximian.
2. Dacia was occupied by the Gepids and Goths, the Rhine –Danube angle by the Alemanni. The other changes of note among the barbarians are the appearance of the Burgundians on the middle Rhine and the disappearance of the Bastarnae who took refuge within the Empire. In Egypt Diocletian withdrew the frontier to the first cataract.

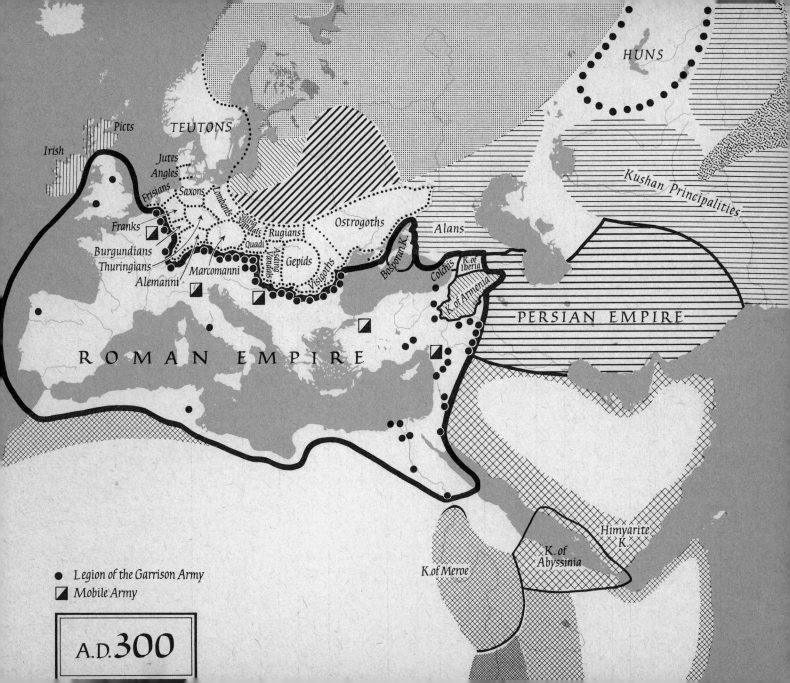

Irish

Picts

TEUTONS

Jutes
Angles
Frisians
Saxons
Lombards

Franks
Burgundians
Thuringians
Alemanni

Marcomanni

Vitina
Vandals
Quadi
Asding
Vandals

Rugians

Gepids

Ostrogoths

Visigoths

Bosporan K.

Alans

Colchis

K. of
Iberia

K. of Armenia

HUNS

Kushan Principalities

PERSIAN EMPIRE

ROMAN EMPIRE

K. of Meroe

K. of
Abyssinia

Himyarite
K.

● Legion of the Garrison Army

◪ Mobile Army

A.D. 300

In 305 Diocletian and Maximian abdicated, Galerius and Constantius succeeded them as Augusti and two new Caesars were appointed. This was the only occasion when the transfer of tetrarchical power went according to plan. On Constantius' death (306) his son Constantine was proclaimed by his troops, and later the same year, Maxentius, the son of Maximian, seized power in Italy. Diocletian had divided the imperial responsibility; now self-declared Augusti divided the Empire. Once rivalry replaced partnership civil war was only a matter of time and in 312 Constantine overthrew Maxentius at the battle of the Milvian bridge just outside Rome. The victory made him master of the West; eleven years later he took over the East too.

If Constantine the Great earned his epithet on the battlefield, he ensured its perpetuation by his patronage of the Christian Church. Perhaps originally only a move to embarrass his enemy, the determined persecutor Galerius, Constantine's Christianity grew with his success till, on his death-bed, he accepted baptism. As the sources for his life are few and tendentious, in the matter of motive you can take your choice between the last bargain of a superstitious man and the final conviction of a cautious one, but the matter is merely biographical for Christianity had won the Empire before it won the Emperor.

In the eastern half of the Empire, where Christians were already a majority, and where officialdom had never identified much with the traditional myths and practices that passed for religion among the Romans, the new faith became the basis for a patriotic feeling among the masses that had hitherto been entirely lacking. Even allowing for the divisive effect of the numerous heresies, the result must have been a very considerable strengthening of the state. And externally the adoption of Christianity by Armenia (303)

88

bound this strategically important land closer to Rome.[1] The Goths also accepted Christianity about this time, though without noticeable improvement. Always the most powerful of the German tribes they soon recuperated from their defeats at the hands of the Illyrian emperors and in the early fourth century the eastern (Ostrogothic) branch rapidly expanded, mainly at the expense of the Slavs. This expansion became explosive under King Ermanarich who extended Ostrogothic hegemony northwards to the Baltic; he also advanced his eastern frontier across the Don, and occupied the Bosporan kingdom, for centuries a sleepy Roman protectorate.

The harmonious division of the Empire was an administrative and military necessity. Constantine's new capital, Constantinople, brought the Greek East into balance with Rome and the Latin West, but his sons were three and the natural bisection of the Empire was postponed until the Constantinian line had ended. The survivor of the three sons, Constantius II, made his nephew Julian his colleague, then within a year he too died. Julian, in an erratic postscript to the dynasty, renounced Christianity, promoted a pedantic paganism, and finally perished, after two years of sole rule, in battle against the Persians (362).

The Constantinians, who were all competent generals, successfully coped with the barbarian invasions that had now become habitual, but their reliance on the mobile army was absolute. The garrison army was allowed to dwindle to a watch-tower militia.[2] Perhaps the expense of two armies had been too great, perhaps the efficiency of the garrison force too low to justify its maintenance; nevertheless the reliance on mobile defence exposed the frontier provinces to continuous warfare. Though the invaders might be crushed, the border-lands became depopulated and their repopulation could only be achieved by the settlement of defeated enemies. This was to be the first scene of the last act.

1. The conversion of the Abyssinians (c.350) was too distant an event to be equally helpful; the Abyssinian destruction of the Kingdom of Meroe was to result if anything in increased restlessness among the Nubians. The Abyssinians also conquered the Yemen at this time; they held it until the Himyarites recovered and expelled them from Arabia in 378.

2. The distribution of the garrison army units, such as they were, corresponds with the line of the frontier, with the addition of two new commands to counter Saxon piracy on the east coast of England and the north coast of France. In Egypt the garrisons lay along the Nile with only a few in the outlying oases.

The stations of the mobile army are unchanged apart from the substitution of Constantinople for Nicomedia. In 362 many units would have been transferred from Europe to the East for the war against Persia.

Irish
Picts
British
Norse
Swedes
Jutes
Danes
Angles
Frisians
Saxons
Lombards
Thuringians
Franks
OSTROGOTHS
Burgundians
Alemann
Silina
Vandals
Rugians
Quadi
Asding
Vandals
Gepids
Marcomanni
Visigoths
Alans
HUNS
Kushan Principalities
Colchis
Iberia
Armenia
PERSIAN EMPIRE

ROMAN EMPIRE

K. of Abyssinia

A.D. 362

The third-century collapse of the Augustan system was financial as well as military; expenditure consistently outran revenue and attempts to conceal the deficit by debasing the coinage only accelerated the inflationary process that finally destroyed the government's credit, hamstrung the administration and paralysed the economy. Reconstruction began with Diocletian. The re-establishment of the currency was obviously contingent on a balanced budget and, in parallel with an attempt at enforcing stable prices by legislation, Diocletian put the whole empire – including Italy – on a new and more exacting scale of taxation. With defence spending at a higher level than ever before the administrative effort needed to obtain a matching income was immense; the empire became a rigid, bureaucrat-ridden society, living under martial law.

Of the many executive innovations of the crisis period the most significant was the division of the empire into Eastern and Western halves. Even when one man ruled both, as happened intermittently to the end of the fourth century, their administrations and finances remained distinct and economically their courses were very different. The East undoubtedly benefited from the split, retaining the taxes and tribute that had previously been remitted to Rome; Egyptian corn was re-routed to Constantinople and the new capital, which got off to a flying start by incorporating the not inconsiderable city of Byzantium, soon grew to metropolitan size. To some extent Constantinople drew trade and population away from the Ionian sea ports, but its creation certainly strengthened the economy of the East as a whole and the urban element in particular. By the date of this map the Eastern cities and the traffic between them had regained the pre-crisis level; Palmyra and Hatra had rebelled against their overlords, respectively Roman and Parthian, and

90

been destroyed, but the silk route flourished and the Sassanids' vigorous promotion of city life must have led to a general increase in traffic between the two empires. The resources were there to pay Diocletian's new taxes.

In the West it was a different story. Rome herself, after fattening on the produce of the entire Mediterranean basin for three hundred years, lost the corn of Egypt, the tribute of the East and even, as the headquarters of the mobile army at Milan became the seat of the Western court and civil government, its capital status and the official expenditure that this had entailed. The city became a backwater, the home of the lost causes of aristocracy and paganism. Italy as a whole shared Rome's eclipse. In the south impoverishment and depopulation had begun even before the reduction to provincial rank; as early as the reign of Augustus Gallic potters were producing a good imitation of Italian ware and the export trade of Campania had gradually dwindled away thereafter. The high cost agriculture of south Italy had similarly declined in face of African and Spanish competition.[1] These troubles were of more than local importance, for of the Western provinces only Italy and Tunisia had ever attained a socio-economic level equivalent to that of the Hellenized East: in the remainder the population was too sparse and too unsophisticated to sustain a city-centred way of life. Cities were founded as a matter of policy, but few became self-supporting; even such apparently successful clusters as Trier, Metz and Mainz in Gaul, and Milan, Verona and Aquileia in the Po valley, depended on the presence of the Gallic and Italian divisions of the mobile army for their prosperity. The failure to urbanize made the West less easy to tax and more expensive to administer. Given another century of patience and encouragement the situation might have improved, but the demands of the military were present and insistent and the consequences of their importunity ruinous.

The factory system never replaced the self-employed artisan in the ancient world because few manufacturing processes needed much capital; their main requirement was skill. Though the Eastern city dwellers, with their long-established standards and unimpaired purchasing power, continued to demand goods of superior workmanship, in the West such tastes were a recent and superficial acquisition. We have seen how quickly Gallic potters learnt to satisfy the local market for Italian-type wares; in Africa we can follow the progress of economic decentralization a stage further, for the Carthaginian copies of imported Roman lamps were themselves replaced by home-made versions, crude but serviceable. The reversion to self-sufficiency and barbarism was all too easy; taxation, most readily inflicted on the city-dweller, encouraged the process. The attempt to convert towns that had run a chronic, but mild, deficit into sources of revenue destroyed them, the citizens simply dispersing across the countryside. Nor was taxation the only force driving them into hiding. The government's price-fixing had made many professions profitless, and its attempts to avoid the economic consequences of its acts by making the practice of such professions obligatory and the liability hereditary, must have created many outlaws. In the Orwellian twilight of the West, citizenship had become slavery and the paradox was completed when serfdom became the free man's aspiration. To protect himself from the summary requisitions of the tax-gatherer the small farmer bought the protection of the local magnate by the gift of his freehold. The Mediterranean ideal of responsible citizenship was replaced by a society living in rural isolation and ignorance, whose stratification in terms of patron

*(continued over)*

1. There is no evidence to support the view that such factors as soil erosion and malaria played any part in precipitating the decline of Italian agriculture, of which they were in all probability a consequence. They would, and in later times certainly did, act against the recovery of abandoned land.

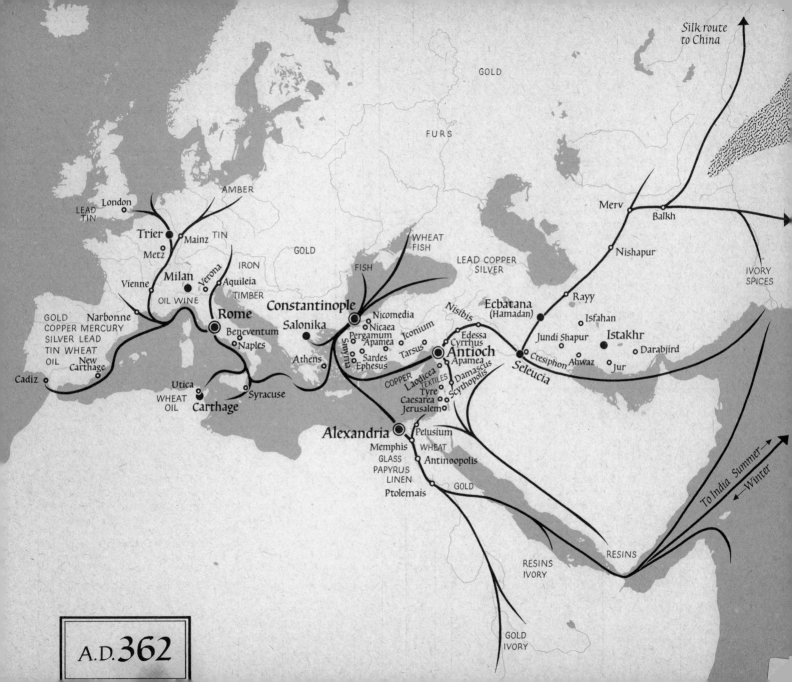

GOLD

Silk route
to China

FURS

GOLD

LEAD
TIN    London

AMBER

Trier    Mainz    TIN

Metz

IRON

Milan    Verona    Aquileia

Vienne    OIL WINE    TIMBER

GOLD

GOLD    Narbonne

COPPER MERCURY

SILVER LEAD

TIN WHEAT

OIL    New

Cadiz    Carthage

Utica    WHEAT
OIL    Carthage

Syracuse

Rome

Beneventum

Naples

Salonika

Constantinople

WHEAT
FISH

FISH

Nicomedia

Nicaea

Pergamum    Iconium

Apamea

Smyrna    Tarsus

Sardes

Athens    Ephesus

LEAD COPPER
SILVER

Nisibis

Edessa

Cyrrhus

Antioch

Apamea

COPPER    Laodicea    TEXTILES

Tyre    Damascus

Caesarea    Scythopolis

Jerusalem

Alexandria    Pelusium

Memphis    WHEAT

GLASS    Antinoopolis

PAPYRUS

LINEN

Ptolemais    GOLD

Ecbatana
(Hamadan)

Ctesiphon

Seleucia

Merv    Balkh

Nishapur

Rayy

Isfahan    Istakhr

Jundi Shapur    Darabjird

Ahwaz

Jur

IVORY
SPICES

RESINS

RESINS
IVORY

To India Summer
Winter

GOLD
IVORY

A.D. 362

(*continued from page 90*)
and client, lord and serf, pre-figured the feudalism of the Middle Ages. Caught in the spiral of dwindling revenue and increasingly rapacious exactions, the West was doomed.

The liberty of thought that was a feature of Mediterranean culture in its best moments had been little in evidence for some time prior to its extinction by Christianity. Even before the third-century crisis, in the materially successful Severan period, there was a noticeable increase in the irrational and histrionic element in Roman life, and this has often been taken to indicate a fundamental intellectual failure which Christianity exploited but did not cause. European historians are mostly hellenophiles and the view of antiquity as a decline presided over by unimaginative Romans from a golden age that was exclusively Greek has apparently become a fixture in historical thinking. The antithesis is of course unfair, reflecting only the scholars' preference for speculation over empiricism, but it does contain the admission that the Greek achievement was itself incomplete and suggests that the root cause of the collapse of classical society was the failure of Greek theory and Roman practice to nourish one another. Speculation ran way beyond the testable and dwindled into metaphysics; technology remained tradition-bound and sluggish. Only the evolution of a scientific stance – one foot inside the boundary of the known, the other just outside – could have guaranteed the superiority, and consequently the integrity, of Mediterranean society, and the world was still too young for that.

So however moving we may find the Greek awakening – the sudden discovery of the question and of the delights of intellectual precision – we must remember that this was an event of the pre-scientific era. It was not the first chord of a majestic theme but something more exciting and less important, a fashion. The golden age is in the eye of the beholder.

(*continued from page 28*)
eastern Indo-European, but overlapping both the western Indo-European and Finno-Ugrian areas – is often said to indicate idea-diffusion rather than migration, it is usual to date the advance of the Indo-Europeans into central Russia to this period. River names reveal that the immigrants were Balts and, indeed, allow an approximate outline to be given for the Balts as a whole. Recognition of the Balts implies the contemporary existence of the Slavs in the zone immediately to the south of the Thraco-Cimmerians on the steppe. As for outlying *battle-axe* finds on the Volga and on the shores of the Gulf of Finland, they may well represent Indo-European (?Balt) migrants. If they do, the intruders must have been absorbed by the Finno-Ugrian natives over the next few centuries. This map and its immediate successors equivocate as to the situation in this intermediate zone; the other new shadings are permanent introductions characterizing definite ethnic groups.

The *bell-beaker/battle-axe* period saw the dissemination of copper working across Europe; it also saw an increase in the relative importance of stock-raising as against crop-raising throughout the continent.

1. A ship that foundered just short of Massilia at about the date of this map was carrying six hundred Neapolitan pots and ten thousand gallons of wine of which four-fifths were Neapolitan. Apart from a few gallons from Rhodes, the rest was Sicilian.

(*continued from page 70*)
the same impulse was at work as early as the fourth century in the advance to Campania. Certainly it was the booming population of their city that sealed the Romans' first conquests. Instead of continuing to dispute her hegemony, the citizens of the neighbouring towns migrated to the new capital, thus confirming her status: Latins and Etruscans alike, Rome's nearer rivals simply disappeared. Although the city fathers opposed the influx and there were repeated efforts to reverse it by programmes of sponsored emigration, nothing could halt this inexorable growth. Again, in later times, we can to some extent understand the impulse behind this: the importation of cheap corn, depriving the mid-Italian farmer of his market and profit, drove him from his village into the city, where he completed the vicious circle by adding his voice to the demand for cheap corn. But why Rome was already so much larger than any other city in Latium or Etruria in the generation after the sack by the Gauls remains a mystery; perhaps the Gauls, by demonstrating the vulnerability of small towns, provided a stimulus to aggregation.

Whatever the nature of her own rocketing expansion as a city, in the early days of her empire Rome did less than nothing for the urbanization of her provinces. True, Spain and Gaul were not yet at the stage for city formation, but in the already developed areas the legions brought disaster. Carthage and Corinth were razed and Syracuse so treated that it never regained its former rank. About Athens the Romans were sentimental – they made her a gift of Delos – but the only cities in the Roman sphere that were really prospering in the mid second century were the Campanian towns, Naples,[1] Puteoli and Capua. Their wine, oil, pottery and metalwork supplied the Italian market, the colonists in the provinces and, as they gradually acquired Roman tastes, the provincials themselves.

# Index

The grid and inset numbers following the names of towns etc. refer to the map on the inside of the back cover. Archaeological cultures are italicized.

bib. = biblical name
class. = classical name
mod. = modern name

95